THE AZURE CLOISTER

Carlos Germán Belli

The Azure Cloister

Thirty-Five Poems

Translated by Karl Maurer

Edited by Christopher Maurer

SWAN
ISLE
PRESS

CHICAGO, 2022

The Complete Poems (*Los versos juntos, 1946-2008*) of **Carlos Germán Belli** (b. 1927) include seventeen books published between 1958 and 2008. A major presence in Peruvian and Latin American Poetry, Belli is the winner of the Casa de las Américas and Pablo Neruda Ibero-American Poetry Award, a Guggenheim grant, and has been nominated for the Nobel Prize.

Karl Maurer (1948-2005) was a Professor of Classics at the University of Dallas, the author of *Interpolation in Thucydides; An Introduction to Robert Frost: A Talk and Notes*; and of translations from Virgil, Jacob Balde, Borges, Sor Juana Inés de la Cruz and other Spanish and Latin authors.

Christopher Maurer is a Professor of Spanish in Boston University

Swan Isle Press, Chicago
© 2021 by Swan Isle Press
© Carlos Germán Belli
Translations © Felipe G. Maurer and Carolina Mia Maurer
Edition and Notes © Christopher Maurer
Printed in the United States of America
First Edition

25   24   23   22   21   1   2   3   4   5

ISBN-13: 978-0-9972287-9-3

Library of Congress Cataloging-in-Publication Data
Names: Belli, Carlos Germán, author. | Maurer, Karl, translator. | Maurer,
    Christopher, editor.
Title: The azure cloister : thirty-five poems / Carlos Germán Belli ; translated
    by Karl Maurer ; edited by Christopher Maurer.
Description: First edition. | Chicago : Swan Isle Press, 2021. | Parallel text in
    Spanish and English. | Includes bibliographical references.
Identifiers: LCCN 2021043829 | ISBN 9780997228793 (paperback)
Subjects: LCSH: Belli, Carlos Germán--Translations into English. | LCGFT:
    Poetry.
Classification: LCC PQ8497.B43 A9813 2021 | DDC 861/.64--dc23
LC record available at https://lccn.loc.gov/2021043829

Swan Isle Press gratefully acknowledges that this edition was made possible,
in part, with generous support from the following:
    BOSTON UNIVERSITY CENTER FOR THE HUMANITIES
    FRIENDS OF LARK
    EUROPE BAY GIVING TRUST

CONTENTS

Notes on Carlos Germán Belli

The Peruvian Carlos Germán Belli (b. 1927) seems to me the greatest living poet of the Spanish language, and perhaps of any language. But his verse has such a sort of purity and such solitude that no one seems to know quite what to make of it. Other poets do not envy him; no one imitates him; and he is almost never translated.

Each of Belli's books makes a sharp queer impression. Both because of the care taken by him in composing each book and because of a kind of interpenetration among the poems (and books) themselves—a certain shameless repetition of themes, images, beloved words, lines, and even poems, as if the poet could not refrain from quoting himself—a book by him is not a mere collection but is itself a poetic work—i.e. the self-analysis of a soul—which fascinates by its purity.

But the purity is noticed later. One is struck first by the language: by a strange inverted word order, tortuous Gongoresque syntax, complex stanza-forms and even diction (*paso horrísono, duro rigor de la pradera helada*) taken from the Spanish Siglo de Oro. Often a line frankly resembles Quevedo or Garcilaso. Moreover, there are certain Nymphs, Zephyrs, Auster and Aquilon, shepherds, fawns, sweet vales, lares, the *planeta, globo* or *orbe*, etc. Thus, for example, we read of a foetus, emerging from the womb:

y abandonar le duele al fin el claustro
en que no rugen ni cierzo ni austro.[1]

and it hurts him to quit for good that cloister,
where no North Wind and South Wind ever roister.

("Poem")

A reader may find this alarming, as if it were some kind of pastiche—some bizarre game. Yet there are strong hints that is impossible: (a) something passionate yet calm in the tone of voice; pithy slang expressions, Americanisms, scientific or technical terms (some of which no other poet would dare to use) interwoven with the archaisms; (c) a kind of grotesque majesty in the imagery, which is hyperbolic to the point of fantasy or dream; and (d) a dark message which at first seems itself exaggerated, but which often is expressed, as here, more simply than by other "poets of absence":

Por este monte abajo cuánto agudo,
ladera tras ladera cual un bólido,
a menos nos venimos para siempre,
del todo donde entronizados fuimos
    al nada que hoy habemos.

Cuán fácil otros van a más sin pena,
centuplicando el todo así boyantes,
como si dellos fuere el sino solo
el alma y cuerpo a tutiplén llenar
    con aire, fuego y agua.

---

1. Spanish text from Carlos Germán Belli, *Los versos juntos, 1946-2008. Poesía completa*, (Seville: Sibilina, S.L.U. and Fundación BBVA, 2008).

En tanto que los otros raudo suben
a la par a este feudo nos venimos,
a derribarnos en sus hondos antros
que así tal vez el horroroso cetro
      del deterioro habremos. [...]

Forever down the mountain how acute
slope after slope and like a shooting star
we come to less forever, from the all
where we enthronèd were, into the nothing
      of what we own today.

How effortlessly others go to more,
centuplicating the all, as buoyantly
as if they had no fate but that of filling
the soul and body both to overflowing
      with air, and fire, and water.

In equal measure as the others rise,
as suddenly, we come into this fiefdom,
to plummeting into its deepest caverns,
so as to own, perhaps, the dreadful sceptre
      of the deterioration. [...]

    This great poem ("Down the Mountain") lacks the irony
that most of his others have; still, all contain the shameless,
stubborn, rather Job-like complaints of a victim who some-
times seems to lack religious faith and seems faced not only by
an incurable social injustice, but by the grimness of an "external
world" which is that of modern physics, and which is devoid of
proper names, local gods, history, and ontological content.

Into this unsacred space, which in his earlier verse is felt in the form of physical pain or hunger, or as an oppressive or vertiginous emptiness, later come certain actual demons. Empty space becomes outer space:

Los extraterrestres

Yo nieto soy de Elvira de la Torre,
y cual ella cercándome hoy diviso
comensales por doquier
ya de garfios crinados, ya de trinches,
y largos cucharones como brazos,
y por lengua una daga,
cual para la más dura vianda en mesa.

Pero no humanos tales raros seres
por afuera luciendo niquelados,
(pues ni del orbe son),
y de hierro por adentro cuánto armados,
tornando en aserrín las antiguas sillas,
después de expoliar fieros
los sándwiches terrestres para siempre. [...]

The Extraterrestrials

I, grandson of Elvira de la Torre,
like her today descry besieging me
  commensals everywhere,
maned now with drag-hooks, now with carving-knives,
and with long ladle-spoons that dangle arm-like,
  and no tongue but a dagger
as for the toughest viands upon the board.

And yet not human are they, such rare beings,
all on the outside gleaming nickel-plated,
  (not of the orb they are),
and inside all of iron oh how armed,
as they reduce the antique chairs to sawdust
when they have sacked, ferocious,
all their terrestrial sandwiches forever.[...]

Now, this poem is only the tip of an iceberg. In Belli the images, though often they are so great and strange that they represent the voice of the poet's soul itself, arise out of the Spanish language. Image and word, from one point of view, are inseparable; yet Belli's entire *oeuvre* (as critics have noticed) is a kind of linguistic "system," in which every image becomes a syntactic sign, a formula, the center of a far-reaching linguistic web. In this, Belli's verse resembles that of Mandelstam. When a new word enters Belli's system, what an adventure for that word! Belli's entire *oeuvre* in fact is nothing but one gigantic sestina. Or to say it another way, each poem, as it is read, rises above the others, but echoes and sums them up, like a cadenza. And because of the exact verbal repetitions, every great image, like those of Mandelstam, has a kind of crystalline depth and each new poem reveals another of its facets.

This revealing of facets cannot be properly illustrated here. One would have to quote at far greater length than is possible here. I give a tiny example, taken at random:

que tal robot dichoso
las gordas letras persiguió jamás
y antes bien *engranaron*
en las dentadas ruedas de su testa...

and such a lucky robot
was not compelled to chase the big block letters
    but they instead *enlocked*
in the enlocking cogwheels of his head...

("*Sublunary Robot*")

e impios bregan para en mí *engranar*
sus cuchillos, sus trinches, sus cucharas...

and struggle godless to *engear* in me
pitilessly their carving knives, their spoons...

("*The Extraterrestrials*")

...pues soy acá cuán célibe,
aguardando que algún herrero *engrane*
un borde mío al hemisferio ajeno,
para que vuele, corra o nade al fin,
    entornillado yo
al aire, tierra o aguas. Así sea.

    for here I am, how celibate,
still waiting for some blacksmith to engear
a rim of mine to the foreign hemisphere,
so as at last to fly, or run, or swim
    and be, thus, tightly bolted
to air, or earth, or water. Be it so!

("*The Transmissions*")

It would be strange to regard this repetition as a "poverty" (as some critics have called it), just as it would be strange to condemn the queer diction or twisted syntax. These things all have the same effect, which is that of turning language, which in prose or in Walt Whitman is so transparent, into a rather opaque "medium" like those of the other arts. As Auden said, "a poem is a well-made verbal object that does honor to the language in which it is written." The meaning that trickles through becomes all the more precious, like that of a lover who speaks by signs or by gifts. By this decorative means, Belli not only is "distanced" from the darkness of his message (which is no less true for that distance), and from the ugliness of present-day speech, but he also imitates the struggle to speak of his own lost, clumsy, rather obsolete soul. That too is an "image." And more than this, one cannot justly ask now of a poet.

These repetitions and this opaqueness have an additional benefit: perhaps the greatest of all. In the so-called art of poetry, which in fact is not an art like the others, because it has no opaque physical medium but works directly with the Word, it is rare to find an ever-deepening, ever surer artistry, comparable to that of a musician or painter. In poetry, every great gain entails a great loss and this is true even of supreme practitioners such as Shakespeare. For example, brilliance is traded for wisdom—or else for an inferior brilliance. In Belli, as with some painters, I, at least, cannot perceive any loss, only an ever greater art; and this is doubtless due in part to his "medium." This change, as well as other, still more precious "developments" in Belli's art and in his "message," it is quite impossible to illustrate.

And Belli's speech is laconic, lapidary, aphoristic. His aphoristic power—for example, take the phrase *el escolar malsano cepo* (p. 24) —is so great that it overshadows even the queer diction. The author himself fondly recalls his own definitions (why not?) and each new book is like a revised anthology of his own aphorisms. And since poetry is nothing but "memorable speech," this procedure is justified.

At the risk of being misunderstood, I would say that Belli's entire art is that of an ironist. "Irony, that language of slaves," as Milosz said. Or to say it another way, Belli is a poet of transcendence, not of immanence, and he has nothing in common with Whitman! He is a lover of terrible subjects distanced by elaborate stanza-forms and rhetorical mannerisms, which are not without humor, yet not without majesty; and among modern poets, there is no one like him.

II

On Translating Belli

He is, of course, prodigiously untranslatable, which is the only good excuse for his utter neglect in this country. In the first place, English obliterates inverted word order and Latinate syntax, not to mention the diction. In the second place, English tends to have fewer syllables ("head" for *cabeza*, "heart" for *corazón*, etc.), so that the meter is hard to keep without padding. But third and worst, the aforementioned repetitions of words—that is, the presence of beloved "key" words which are, themselves, the greatest artistic "images"—are hard to keep because the meaning of each of them changes with the context. But if I translate a word differently in different places, I have risked losing the huge "sestina" of Belli's art.

He is one of the greatest of modern poets; but when translated literally, his message looks too merely bitter, whereas in fact it is anything but that. Belli might seem a Manichee, alienated from the Creation, from the flesh and from his own body, as if the world itself (as Robert Frost said, "the whole goddam machinery") were the cause of the mischief. But this is not the case. That Belli acquiesces in the myth of the Fall is shown (a) by memories of Paradise that are not rhetorical and that are scattered throughout his verse (*el todo donde entronizados fuimos*; "the all where we enthronèd were"); (b) by his awareness of his own sin as the origin of evil (*Perdón, papá, mamá, porque mi yerro...* / "Sorry, papa, mama, because my error..."); (c) by his constant humor, which is not mere irony and which pervades every line of his verse, so that his hyperbolical complaints and condemnations are, indeed, frankly hyperbolical; (d) by the beauty of his linguistic art which affirms the order of the world.

Only this last point needs explaining. Belli's elaborately formal verse, which is austere and devoid of sensuousness but not of architectonic and musical power, is not that of a gnostic "symbolist" trying, like Mallarmé, to move *a realibus a realiora*. In his case, the paradise adumbrated by the verse-form does not belong to the artist, the adept who penetrates there; it belongs to each reader, and is located not in the future but in the past. This is hard to "prove" though it is obvious in the mere tone of voice:

> Yo nieto soy de Elvira de la Torre,
> y cual ella cercándome hoy diviso
> comensales por doquier...
>
> I, grandson of Elvira de la Torre,
> like her today descry besieging me
>   commensals everywhere...

> ("*The Extraterrestrials*")

Belli's incomparably rich tone of voice (it is "comparable" in fact with the voices of Auden and Mandelstam—they alone equal him in this) is already one of the glories of the Spanish language.

In Belli's formalism there is also nostalgia. I mean nostalgia not only for what was lost in the past. Belli's baroque art, his stanzaic, highly plastic and stereoscopic art is the creation, by a man who owns nothing, of interior space: stanzaic palaces, rooms, stairways, corridors, vistas. Belli's Peruvian "owners" inhabit houses which are, no doubt, far less impressive than the interior of the octopus in "*Bolo de pulpo*" ("Bolus of an Octopus"). Belli's love of stanza-forms, of stereoscopic, Latinate syntax, which examines every object from all three sides, betrays therefore a love of the world, and it is also the poet's indispensable sense of his own rightness. As Mandelstam said, "Poetry is the sense of being right"; and as Mandelstam also said, apropos of the architect, "the builder puts one stone on another and says, I build. That means, I am right."

III
On Belli's Shameless Repetitions!

It is not so much (though there *is* something of this in all formal verse) that he likes to test every new image, or thing, in "laboratory conditions." He seems, rather, a lover of language who naively believes that it *does* contain and is stubbornly concealing a revelation. (Thus, according to him, "Poetry is communication with the unknown.").

He is one who trusts language—which he knows to be a vessel of wisdom, a memory of philosophy and scripture— more than he trusts other people, his own heart, his nervous system or even his great images. And thus he has the air of someone constantly trying combinations of words, as if he were solving a puzzle.

Thus, a quoter!—one who loves to repeat his own words, and those of others. A "humble" man, because of his fascination with certain predecessors—half a dozen, say—whom he reads and rereads.

One who is struck by the strangeness of his own art: one who reads and rereads himself with great pleasure. One who knows his own work by heart.

And why should anybody rewrite what was well said? His aphorisms are often *perfect* and succeed in being "memorable speech" which is poetry. These lines are immortal:

> El rollizo pie ajeno
> su planta en vez del vasto suelo posa
> sobre el delgado chasis de mi cuello...

> And someone's chubby foot,
> instead of treading ample earth, is pressing
> upon the fragile chassis of my neck...

> *("The Cornucopia")*

Perhaps he is often tired of his "theme and variations" (as he is of his life) and longs for something altogether new. But he can never just "turn over a new leaf," because of his fascination with the strangeness of what he has written.

The bored reader of Belli's monotonous work is tempted to ask him, "Ah, why don't you just change your life?" Belli is the opposite of the man of whom Tolstoy said, "When a man tries to go to sleep on an anthill, and is bitten repeatedly, he doesn't protest and kick at the pricks, he gets up and walks away."

It is not Belli but his art that is changing place. Discussion of a living poet's "development" is always oppressive, even when tactful, and usually wrong. But let the reader himself compare the early poem *"Frunce el feto su frente"* (p. 18) with the following more recent one; for in a certain sense the theme is the same:

El nudo

Esa increíble infinitud del orbe
no codicio ni un mínimo pedazo,
mas sí el espacio de tu breve cuerpo
donde ponerme al fin a buen recaudo,
en el profundo de tus mil entrañas,
que enteras preservaste para mí.
Al diablo el albedrío de la vida,
sumo don de los hados celestiales,
y nada más que estar en ti prefiero
sujeto a tu carnal y firme lazo,
que si vas a las últimas estrellas
contigo ir paso a paso yo también.
Es así el vivir día y noche siempre
bien atado a ti con el carnal nudo
aunque en verdad del todo libremente
pues de la tierra al cielo voy y vengo.

(8 de enero de 1986)
Bajo el sol de la medianoche rojo, 1990

The Knot

That incredible infinity of the orb
I do not covet nor its merest piece,
but do the brief space in it of your body,
wherein to put myself at last in custody,

in the profoundness of your thousand entrails,
that you preserved entirely just for me.
The Devil, then, may keep this life's free will,
that sweetest gift of the celestial fates,
since I choose nothing but to be in you,
subjected to your taut and carnal slip-knot,
and if you travel to the farthest stars,
footstep by footstep with you to go too.
So living is by day, by night, forever
tied tightly to you by the carnal knot,
although in truth so free of everything
as I go skywards, earthwards, to and fro.

(January 8, 1986)

Karl Maurer, 1987

CARLOS GERMÁN BELLI

Asir la forma que se va

Hay quienes creen en la Divinidad únicamente por el pavor ante la possible nada. Igualmente hay quienes adoran la forma artística ante el temor de que termine por desintegrarse para siempre. Pero en este caso la angustia no es la única causa, sino que a la vez hay una tácita devoción sensorial, tan antigua como los propios objetos estéticos. Es la fe en la forma, no por el riesgo del vacío, sino por el puro placer de disfrutarla. Igualmente como cuando se adora a la Divinidad por sí misma, y aun si no existiera. En realidad, ni espuria, ni imputable a barrocos o parnasianos. No hay que avergonzarse de ella. No hay que reducirla a la prostración. Obrar así no es otra cosa que renegar de nuestro continente. Porque los cuerpos en que moramos también poseen un contorno, también una estructura donde se encuentran en perfecto orden y concierto los secretos órganos vitals. Aferrémonos a ella, como nos aferramos a nuestra forma corporal, ante el embate del tiempo, ante la aproximación de la ineludible muerte.

Taking Hold of the Form That Flees

Some believe in divinity solely because they are terrified by possible nothingness. In the same way some adore artistic form out of fear that it will end up disintegrating forever. But anguish is not the only cause of this; there is also a tacit devotion of the senses as old as the aesthetic objects themselves. This is the faith in form not from the risk of the void, but from the pure pleasure of enjoying it. This happens in the same way in which Divinity is adored for itself, even were it not to exist. In reality form is not spurious, not attributable merely to baroque or Parnassian decadents. There must be no shame on account of it. It must not be made to abase itself. That would be to disown our container. For the bodies in which we dwell possess a contour, also a structure, where the secret vital organs are found in perfect order and agreement. Let us hold fast to it, as we hold fast to our bodily form against the attack of time, against the approach of inevitable death.

Poema

Nuestro amor no está en nuestros respectivos
y castos genitales, nuestro amor
tampoco en nuestra boca, ni en las manos:
todo nuestro amor guárdase con pálpito
bajo la sangre pura de los ojos.
Mi amor, tu amor esperan que la muerte
se robe los huesos, el diente y la uña,
esperan que en el valle solamente
tus ojos y mis ojos queden juntos,
mirándose ya fuera de sus órbitas,
más bien como dos astros, como uno.

Poemas, 1958

Poem

Our love is not in our respective
chaste genitals; our love is not
in our mouth, either, nor in hands:
all our love throbbing keeps itself
beneath the pure blood of the eyes.
My love, your own love, expect that death
will steal bones, tooth and fingernail;
they hope that in the valley only
your eyes, and my eyes, still conjoined,
free of their sockets, watch each other
not like two stars, but like one star.

Variaciones para mi hermano Alfonso

I
(casi soneto)

Para tu mudanza, ¿dónde habrá un suelo
de claro polvo y cálido recodo,
en que tus breves pies con tierno modo
equilibren la sangre de tu cuerpo?

O para tu vuelo, ¿cuándo habrá un viento
que llegue a tu costado como un soplo
y te traslade de uno a otro polo,
pasando el edificio, el valle, el cielo?

Pues estás como dura ostra fijo,
sin que nadie te llame y te descorra
el plumaje del ave, hermano mío.

¿Por qué no llega la luz hasta el umbral
de tus huesos para que tus pies corran
por primera vez sobre el propio mar?

Poemas, 1958

Variations for My Brother Alfonso

1
(almost a sonnet)

For you to move, when will there be a floor
of brilliant dust, some warm and cozy nook
wherein your brief feet in a tender manner
will put your body's blood in equilibrium?

For you to fly, when will there be a wind
that at your side arrives so like a breath,
translating you from one pole to another,
passing the building, valley-floor, the sky?

For tightly as an oyster you are stuck
where no one calls, no one unfolds for you
the plumage of a bird.

Why does not light come even to the sill
of your poor bones so that your feet can run,
for the first time, upon the very sea?

Una desconocida voz

Una desconocida voz me dijo:
"no folgarás con Filis, no, en el prado,
si con hierros te sacan
del claustro luminoso, feto mío";
y ahora que en este albergue arisco
encuéntrome ya desde varios lustros
pregunto por qué no fui despeñado,
desde el más alto risco,
por tartamudo o cojo o manco o bizco.

¡Oh hada cibernética! 1962

Un Unknown Voice

An unknown voice told me
"thou shalt not wanton with Phyllis in the meadow, no,
though iron fingers pull you from the radiant womb."
Now, after years in this hostile hotel,
my question is
why didn't they get rid of me, fling me
off some high crag
as stammerer, or cripple, or one-armed, cross-eyed creature.

¡Oh padres, sabedlo bien!

¡Oh padres, sabedlo bien:
el insecto es intransmutable en hombre,
mas el hombre es transmutable en insecto!,
¿acaso no pensabais, padres míos,
cuando acá en el orbe sin querer matabais
un insecto cualquiera,
que hallábase posado oscuramente
del bosque en el rincón más manso y lejos,
para no ser visto por los humanos
ni en el día ni en la noche,
no pensabais, pues, que pasando el tiempo
algunos de vuestros hijos
volveríanse en inermes insectos,
aun a pesar de vuestros mil esfuerzos
para que todo el tiempo
pesen y midan como los humanos?

¡Oh hada cibernética! 1962

O parents, know this well!

O parents, know this well!–
the insects cannot mutate into humans,
but humans do mutate back into insects!;
and parents, did you not perhaps foresee,
when on this orb, not meaning to, you killed
    some insect, any at all
that was astutely nesting in the dimness
of a remote and safe spot in the woods
so it would not be seen by humans, either
    by daylight or at night,–
did you not think then, that as time went by
    several of your own children
would soon regress into defenceless insects,
even despite the thousand pains you took
    to ensure that they would always
have the same weight and measurements as humans?

En saliendo del vientre

En saliendo del vientre tu canilla
no tuvo ni una astilla
de pie ni tu garguero
una astilla de lengua,
mas ¿por qué otros pie y lengua de lucero
desde el vientre tuvieron sin más mengua
para andar, para hablar?
Cuántas deslizaduras has mirado
otras firmes canillas al pasar,
cuando entre pitos gamo raudo cruza,
aun más que el fuerte viento que le azuza;
y cuánta lengua parlera
se menea aunque el dueño no lo quiera,
día y noche, por quítame esa paja;
y tú te enciendes, te asas bajo el cuero
al ver que ante zagala no desgaja
ni una sola palabra el garguero.

¡Oh hada cibernética! 1962

12

In leaping from the womb

In leaping from the womb, your shin had not
   one splinter of a foot
   nor was there in your throat
   one splintered bit of tongue,
but why did others from the womb possess
without decrease a shining tongue and foot
   whereby to walk and speak?
How many other slippings have you watched
   as other firm shins passed,
when between whistles a swift deer would cross
still stronger than the strong wind that excites it;
   and how the wagging tongue
keeps moving though its owner may not want to,
by day and night for no reason at all
and you would burn, would roast beneath the skin
on seeing that before the shepherdess
your throat would not cough up a single word.

En Bética no bella

Ya calo, crudos zagales desta Bética
no bella, mi materia, y me doy cuenta
que de abolladuras ornado estoy
por faenas que me habéis señalado
tan solo a mí y a nadie más ¿por qué?;
mas del corzo la priesa privativa
ante el venablo, yo no podré haber,
o que el seso se me huya de sus arcas
por el cerúleo claustro, pues entonces
ni un olmo habría donde granjear
la sombra para Filis, o a mis vástagos,
o a Anfriso tullido, hermano mío;
pero no cejaré, no, aunque no escriba
ni copule ni baile en esta Bética
no bella, en donde tantos años vivo.

¡Oh hada cibernética! 1962

In Unbeautiful Betis

I now descry, cruel shepherds of this Betis
not beautiful, my substance, and I notice
that I have been adorned somehow with bruises
from drudgery that you have assigned to me,
only to me, and to no other (why?),
but the peculiar quickness of the stag
before the hunting-spear I cannot have,
nor from its strongbox can my brain escape
to the cerulean cloister, since I sense
that there no elm is, under which to gather
the shade for Phyllis, or for sons of mine
or for brother, paralyzed Anfriso;
but yield? —I will not, though I may not write
or mate, or dance, in this unbeautiful
Betis wherein I live so many years.

A mi hermano Alfonso

Pues tanto el leño cuanto el crudo hierro
del cepo que severo te avasalla,
unidos cual un órgano hasta las plantas,
no solo a flor de cuero,
mas sí en el lecho de tu propio tuétano,
que te dejan cual ostra
a la faz del orbe así arraigado;
y el leve vuelo en fin
que en el cerúleo claustro siempre ejerce
el ave más que el claustro desalada,
¿cuándo a ti llegará?,
mientras abajo tú en un aprisco solo
no mueves hueso alguno
ni agitas ya la lengua
para llamar al aire;
pues en el orbe todo viene y va
al soplo de la vida,
que pródigo se torna
para muchos y a no más otros pocos
áspero, vano o nada para siempre.

El píe sobre el cuello, 1964

To My Brother Alfonso

Since both the timber and the cruël iron
of the severe stocks keeping you a vassal
are joined to you too snugly, like an organ,
   from the neck to the footsoles,
   not only on your hide
but even in the channels of your marrow,
   and leave you like an oyster
rooted but in the surface of the world;
   oh when will that light flight
that any bird more rapid than the South Wind
enjoys forever, in its azure cloister,—
   when will it come to you?,
if far below it you inside a sheep-pen
   do not move even a bone
   nor agitate your tongue
   to call out to the air;
since everything sublunar comes and goes
   at the least breath of life,
   that spends so lavishly
on many but for others, only a few,
is rough or empty or for ever, nothing.

Poema

Frunce el feto su frente
y sus cejas enarca cuando pasa
del luminoso vientre
al albergue terreno,
do se truecan sin tasa
la luz en niebla, la cisterna en cieno;
y abandonar le duele al fin el claustro,
en que no rugen ni cierzo ni austro,
y verse aun despeñado
desde el más alto risco,
cual un feto no amado,
por tartamudo o cojo o manco o bizco.

El pie sobre el cuello, 1964

18

Poem

The foetus screws his face,
brows arches, when from in the radiant womb,
which is his proper space,
he comes to rent in time
this his sublunar room,
where light is cloud and where that cistern, slime;
and it hurts him to quit for good that cloister,
where no North Wind and South Wind ever roister,
and find himself even shoved
from the earth's highest crag,
like some foetus unloved
for stuttering, squinting, having feet that drag.

Labio leporino

Este mundo que una boca es de lobo
y erizada aun de leporino labio,
cuya hendidura nunca la rellenan
ni los montes más altos de la tierra,
por ventura hasta ahora no es lanzado,
cual desalado alimenticio bolo,
hacia el sideral buche más remoto;
porque usos son en este mundo ajeno,
que el feto que hasta acá llegar consigue,
con leporino labio cuán hendido,
despeñado es al cuarto mes o sexto,
para que los despojos de su cuerpo,
¡ay! acaso rellenen esta grieta
al fin del grande leporino labio.

Por el monte abajo, 1966

Hare-lip

This wolf's mouth of a world, that bristles even
with a hare-lip, whose gap the highest mountains
of earth cannot stop up, by luck has not,
like an unsalted alimentary bolus,
been shot to the remotest starry maw,
since in this strange world it is customary
for any foetus that has got this far
but grins from a hare-lip, to be out-flung
in the fourth month or sixth, so that its corpse
will stop the crack at the end of that hare-lip.

La tortilla

Si luego de tanto escoger un huevo,
y con él freír la rica tortilla
sazonada bien con sal y pimienta,
y del alma y cuerpo los profundos óleos
para que por fin el garguero cruce
y sea ya el sumo bolo alimenticio
albergado nunca en humano vientre,
¡qué jeringa! si aquella tortilla
segundos no más de ser comida antes,
repentinamente una vuelta sufra
en la gran sartén del azar del día,
cual si un invisible tenedor filoso
le pinche y le coja su faz recién frita,
el envés poniendo así boca arriba,
no de blancas claras ni de yemas áureas,
mas un emplasto sí de mortal cicuta.

Por el monte abajo, 1966

The Omelette

If after so much choosing of an egg,
as one is frying the delicious omelette,
well-seasoned with a shake of salt and pepper
and deep oils of the body and the soul,
so that at last it can descend the gullet
and be the perfect alimentary bolus,
that never sheltered in a human belly,
ah, what a nuisance! if that omelette
seconds, no more, before being gobbled up,
abruptly suffered an incautious flip
in the big pan of chance of any day
as if a fork invisible but deft
had nabbed it, filched its recently fried face
and left thus facing-up an underside
made not of brilliant whites and golden yolks,
but an emplaster, yes, of deadly hemlock.

Robot sublunar

¡Oh sublunar robot!
por entre cuya fúlgida cabeza
la diosa Cibernética
el pleno abecé humano puso oculto,
cual indeleble sello,
en los craneales arcas para siempre;

envídiolo yo cuánto
porque en el escolar malsano cepo
por suerte se vio nunca
un buen rato de su florida edad,
ni su cráneo fue polvo
en los morteros de la ilustración,

que tal robot dichoso
las gordas letras persiguió jamás,
y antes bien engranaron
en las dentadas ruedas de su testa,
no más al concebirlo
el óvulo fabril de la mecánica;

y más lo envidio yo,
porque a sí mismo bástase seguro,
y ágil cual deportista,
de acá para acullá expedito vive,
sin el sanguíneo riego
del ayer, hoy, mañana ineludible.

Por el monte abajo, 1966

Sublunary Robot

Oh sublunary robot!
inside the nicely gleaming head of whom
   the goddess Cybernetica
has hidden the whole human A B C,
   like an enduring seal
upon his cranial strongboxes forever;

   how much I envy him,
since by good luck he never had to bear
   unhealthy schoolboy stocks
and crush the very blossom of his childhood,
   or let his skull be dust
in the mortaria of enlightenment;

   and such a lucky robot
was not compelled to chase the big block letters
   but they instead engaged
the interlocking cogwheels of his head,
   the instant when the fabrile
ovula of mechanic art conceived him;

   and envy him still more
in that he self-suffices; worriless
   and nimble, like an athlete,
lives unimpeded here and yon, without
   the circulating blood
of yesterday, today, doom-filled tomorrow.

Por el monte abajo

Por este monte abajo cuánto agudo,
ladera tras ladera cual un bólido
a menos nos venimos para siempre,
del todo donde entronizados fuimos
  a la nada que habemos.

Cuán fácil otros van a más sin pena,
centuplicando el todo así boyantes,
como si dellos fuere el sino solo
el alma y cuerpo a tutiplén llenar
  con aire, fuego y agua.

En tanto que los otros raudo suben,
a la par a este feudo nos venimos,
a derribarnos en sus hondos antros
que así tal vez el horroroso cetro
  del deterioro habremos.

Bien si poquillos seres no más somos,
el final punto no es ser cosa chica,
que por el mundo tantas hay dispersas,
pues nuestro caso grave más se torna
  por tales agrias cuestas.

Por restregarnos peña a peña siempre,
cual casi nadie en este crudo siglo,
que nuestro estado no es tan solo ya
mudado a menos, cosa chica o polvo,
  sino nada y más nada.

Por el monte abajo, 1966

Down the Mountain

Forever down the mountain how acute
slope after slope and like a shooting star
we come to less forever, from the all
where we enthronèd were, into the nothing
       of what we own today.

How effortlessly others go to more,
centuplicating the all, as buoyantly
as if they had no fate but that of filling
the soul and body both to overflowing
       with air, and fire, and water.

In equal measure as the others rise,
as suddenly, we come into this fiefdom,
to plummeting into its deepest caverns,
so as to own, perhaps, the dreadful sceptre
       of the deterioration.

Though we are tiny creatures now, not more,
the final point is not being something small,
such as about the world are many scattered,
since our case takes an even graver turn
       about such severe slopes

from our being scoured so, crag on crag forever,
like almost no one in this savage century,
and our estate and state is not so much
reduced to less, a tiny thing or dust,
       as into more of nothingness.

Los estigmas

En los retrovisores espejuelos
de mi flamante coche día a día
por el arrabal del burdel al paso,
de mudanzas un gris camión horrible
llamado "Los Estigmas" yo diviso,
cuyos focos cual mortecinos ojos,
por entre la neblina de la noche,
en perseguirme nunca cejan fieros,
cual si mi chasis óptima región
y convenible como pocos fuera
a las atrocidades del defecto
o al tirano motor envejecido,
que bajo su gobierno así se yace
ya fuera de la pista, ya sin ruedas.

Sextinas y otros poemas, 1970

The Stigmas

In both the rear-view mirrors
of my resplendent car day every day
when I go through the brothel neighborhood
I notice a horrible gray moving-van,
  "The Stigmas" called, whereof
   the headlights like dead eyes
   through the nocturnal fog
so fiercely do not cease to follow me,
as though my chassis were their optimum
vicinity, convenient like few others
for the atrocity of a sudden defect
or for the tyranny of the ageing engine,
and under its regime were lying thus
already off the track, and without wheels.

Silva antibiótica

Desta antibiótica tableta
cuándo un fugaz efecto al fin siquiera,
si en los arcanos horizontes gira
cual la luna en el cielo,
que aquicito nomás
al encubierto en tanto
el patógeno troglodita aprieta
las uvas del racimo corporal,
cuánto forzudamente,
más que aquilón a amarillas hojas.
Que vengan los efectos
a prisa cual la liebre,
antes que el dia mude en negra noche,
y a vivir empecemos
en un puntito atroz,
flotando acá, flotando allá fiero
por entre las moléculas
de la gran antibiótica tableta,
en vano día y noche recetada
para no eternizar
estos que somos hoy cien mil patógenos.

Sextinas y otros poemas, 1970

Antibiotic Silva

This antibiotic tablet– O, when will it
have any at least ephemeral effect
if in the arcane horizons it is spinning
   like the moon in the sky,
    while meanwhile, just a little
    farther on, out of sight
the troglodytic pathogen is pressing
the grapes of the corporeal raceme
   with how immense a force,
more than the North Wind presses yellow leaves?
   Let the effects arrive,
   O quickly, like a rabbit
before the daylight changes to black night,
   and we begin to live
   in an atrocious pointlet
that darts now hither, and now thither, fiercely
   among the molecules
of the immense antibiotic tablet
that is prescribed in vain all day and night
   so as not to eternize
these hundred thousand pathogens that we are.

El uso del talón

Este talón, ¡oh hi de aire!, hoy por hoy aún pequeño,
los hados por ventura lindamente te han dado,
a prisa para andar como otros sobre el suelo,
con arreglo a las leyes del globo sublunar;
porque todo es cuestión de talón, ¡oh hi de aire!,
que quien lo tiene no rompido puede andar
y al seno entrar del valle y recoger después
ras con ras con la grey el pan llevar del suelo;
mas la memoria siempre en el precepto fija
de nunca hollar jamás con el calcañal propio
ni al hombre, ni la flor, ni el insecto. Así sea.

Sextinas y otros poemas, 1970

The Use of the Heel

This heel, oh, son of air! today still small,
the fates, by chance, have given you prettily,
to tread the ground with, rapidly, like others
obeying laws of the sublunar globe;
for, son of air! the heel is everything,
and whoso has not broken his can enter
into the valley's bosom, and thereafter
beside the herd, gather the corn and wheat
but fasten memory always on the precept:
not ever, under one's own heel, to trample
the man, the flower, the insect. Be it so.

Los extraterrestres

Yo nieto soy de Elvira de la Torre,
y cual ella cercándome hoy diviso
comensales por doquier
ya de garfios crinados, ya de trinches,
y largos cucharones como brazos,
y por lengua una daga,
cual para la más dura vianda en mesa.

Pero no humanos tales raros seres
por afuera luciendo niquelados,
(pues ni del orbe son),
y de hierro por adentro cuánto armados,
tornando en aserrín las antiguas sillas,
después de expoliar fieros
los sándwiches terrestres para siempre.

Ya al alba compartir la sublunar
de roble mesa rústica me obligan
los desconsiderados
marcianos o lunares comensales,
o qué sé yo de qué planeta ajeno,
y mi ración se llevan,
luego de arar de miga en miga yo.

Si bien nada boyante porque iré
a la tumba seguro con gran gula,
sin dilación me asaltan,
e impíos bregan para en mí engranar
sus cuchillos, sus trinches, sus cucharas,
que si tan ruin estado,
¡qué expolian, qué me trinchan, qué saquean!

Sextinas y otros poemas, 1970

The Extraterrestrials

I, grandson of Elvira de la Torre,
like her today descry besieging me
  commensals everywhere,
maned now with drag-hooks, now with carving-knives,
and with long ladle-spoons that dangle arm-like,
  and no tongue but a dagger
as for the toughest viands upon the board.

And yet not human are they, such rare beings,
all on the outside gleaming nickel-plated,
  (not of the orb they are),
and inside all of iron oh how armed,
as they reduce the antique chairs to sawdust
when they have sacked, ferocious,
all their terrestrial sandwiches forever.

At dawn already me they bid assist
at their sublunar oaken rustic table,
  the inconsiderate
commensals, Martian, or it could be lunar,
or, what do I know from what foreign planet,
  but with my portion make off
when I have plowed from one crumb to another.

And though not buoyant since I go securely
unto the tomb myself a hopeless glutton,
  on me they set forthwith
and struggle godless to engear in me
pitilessly their carving knives, their spoons,
  and though so mean the estate
how they despoil it, me how carve, how plunder.

Canción primera

Estas dos sin par rosas en un tris
de ser baldadas lianas por el suelo,
o en los perfectos pétalos luciendo
el contorno de un labio leporino,
y aun afiladas garras como ramas
a lo largo de un encorvado tallo,
o el imperio del bulbo
en fin avasallando
el buen olor del pétalo;
que si en caso hipotético así fuera,
y no esmaltadas rosas como hoy son,
cuál jardín en su seno las tendría
si del lilio hasta el heno
todo sería no más cardo esquivo.

O bien las ambas tórtolas completas
en las nubes aparecido hubieran,
de alas y patas feamente mochas,
y un cuerpo solo con cabeza y pico,
que de volátil mude en ser campal,
cayendo al bajo suelo cual serpiente,
en tanto el cielo arriba
de alguna ufana tórtola
el usufructo sea;
mas ni llorar su vida al ras del risco,
pues menos que el ofidio existirían,
tanto como un corpúsculo invisible,
y ni silbo y ni son,
y ni a rastras ni vuelo y casi nada.

First Song

These two so peerless roses so in danger
of being lianas crippled on the ground,
or of displaying in their perfect petals,
perhaps, the contour of a bad harelip,
and even piercing talons that, like branches,
sprout up and down a curving stem; or else
  the empire of the bulb
  that, in the end, envassals
  the good smell of the petal, –
if, hypothetically, they became like that,
and not the enameled roses that they are,
what garden in its bosom would preserve them
  if from lily to hay
it all were nothing but evasive thistle?

Or if that pair of perfect turtledoves
up in the clouds were suddenly to appear
with hideously crippled wings and legs,
and, for a body, only head and beak,
mutating from sky-creature to field-creature,
falling, like serpents of the lowly earth,
  (while meanwhile sky above
  is the luxuriant realm
  of some proud turtledove),
and not even mourn their life amid the crags,
since now they'd less exist than does a snake,
and like an imperceptible corpuscle
  be neither hiss nor sound,
and neither crawl nor flight, and almost nothing.

Acá la arcilla como rosa y tórtola
a la par en el sino cada cual,
tan a mil maravillas para siempre,
cuanto en peligro sucesivamente
de gelatina, cieno, grisú o roca,
o todo a la vez, híbrido primero,
cuya confusa mezcla
ni imaginarse alcanza
al verse hoy feliz,
a punto de mudar en cambio toda,
con un divino soplo de por medio
el natural estado en dulce carne,
cuando al revés bien pudo
menos que arcilla ser eternamente.

Si cada cual en riesgo
de híbrido más que el otro,
Canción mía, partid de una vez ya,
que en tris estáis también,
de no ser tal jamás,
sino clo, guau, miau, mu.

GRATIAS DEO

Sextinas y otros poemas, 1970

But here the clay, —like rose and turtledove,
they being all three equal in their fate,
so marvelously perfectly forever,
all so at risk of being successively
mere jelly, merest mud, mere gas or rock,
or all of these at once, a striking hybrid
      whose confused mixture never
      can even imagine seeing
      itself today as happy,
so on the verge of changing utterly
by virtue of a single divine breath
      its natural estate,—
may well be less than clay eternally.

      If each is more in danger
      of hybrids than the others,
ah, once for all, depart, O simple Song
      that are within an inch
      of not being anything
      but caw, bow-wow, miao, moo.

GRATIAS DEO

Los engranajes

A Enrique Molina

Por ningún lado puedo mirar aún
los modales del engranaje finos,
aunque más día y noche aquí los busque
entre miles de máquinas flamantes,
que la fábrica cada rato engendra
por aligerar el trajín del globo;
mas en vano ya fuera
si acaso descubriera acá en la vida
el perfecto engranaje codiciado,
tarde sería para ensamblar todo,
que como piezas sueltas
del cuerpo y alma cuánto quedaría.

Estas grandes máquinas ya dos siglos
sus invenciones nunca ceder quieren,
ocultando a los austros celocísimas
la cerúlea mecánica que gira
cada sinfin tornillo del planeta,
bien de hierro inoxidable, bien de carne;
y a quién elegirán
estas que esquivas son hasta la muerte,
más que vírgenes bellas pudorosas,
guardando bajo tutelares níqueles
el pubis del piñón,
que no engrana con desdentada rueda.

The Transmissions

For Enrique Molina

On no side can I ever see as yet
the refined manners of the gear-transmission,
though every day and night I search for them
among the thousands of brand new machines,
that factories every second generate
to alleviate the bustle of the globe;
   but it would be in vain
if we perhaps discovered here, in life,
the perfect so much coveted transmission;
yes, too late to assemble everything,
   since there would still remain
how much of soul and body, like loose pieces.

These big machines, for two whole centuries,
unwilling to surrender their inventions,
have jealously kept hidden from the South winds
that deep-blue mechanism that rotates
every unceasing worm-gear of the planet,
whether of stainless metal, or of flesh;
   and for whomso they choose,
are more evasive even until death,
than are the loveliest most modest virgins;
protecting under tutelary nickel
   the pubis of a pinion
that never will engage a toothless wheel.

Así me paso día y noche siempre,
tentando por doquier de coronar
los actos cotidianos intrincados,
y alguna vez en el mundano vientre
de un simple mecanismo entrar feliz
para alimentar yo también al globo;
y si andando los años,
las tuercas mías no embragaren nada,
cómo quedaré, ¡ay Dios!, desconectado,
más mísero que bruto, piedra, planta,
quienes ufanos viven,
cada cual cuán seguro en sus reinos.

Ya poquito siquiera engargantarme
a la invisible rueda de los astros,
al fin a la par del tornillo aquel,
que nace, vive y muere inoxidable,
suavemente cual amarilla seda,
por ordenanza de los cielos ciega;
pues soy acá cuán célibe,
aguardando que algún herrero engrane
un borde mío al hemisferio ajeno,
para que vuele, corra o nade al fin,
entornillado yo
al aire, tierra o aguas. Así sea.

Sextinas y otros poemas, 1970

And so I suffer day and night, forever
attempting, every which way, to enwreath
all my quotidian intricated actions,
and sometimes into the sublunar belly
of a simple mechanism, to enter happily,
so that I, too, can nourish all the globe.
    And if, as years go by,
my bolts no longer couple or enlock,
how shall I stay –O good grief!—disconnected,
more wretched than the savage, stones, or plants
    that live contentedly,
each in its kingdom wholly free from worry.

A little bit, at least, to engear myself
with the invisible wheel of the stars,
equal at last to the aforesaid wormscrew,
that is born, lives, and dies as stainless steel,
as smoothly as a piece of yellow silk,
by a blind ordinance of the heavens;
    for here I am, how celibate,
still waiting for some blacksmith to engear
a rim of mine to the foreign hemisphere,
so as at last to fly, or run, or swim
    and be, thus, tightly bolted
to air, or earth, or water. Be it so!

Sextina de los desiguales

Un asno soy ahora, y miro a yegua,
bocado del caballo y no del asno,
y después rozo un pétalo de rosa,
con estas ramas cuando mudo en olmo,
en tanto que mi lumbre de gran día
el pubis ilumina de la noche.

Desde siempre amé a la secreta noche,
exactamente igual como a la yegua,
una esquiva por ser yo siempre día,
y la otra por mirarme no más asno,
que ni cuando me cambio en ufano olmo
conquistar puedo a la exquisita rosa.

Cuánto he soñado por ceñir a rosa,
o adentrarme en el alma de la noche,
mas solitario como día u olmo
he quedado y aun ante rauda yegua,
inalcanzable en mis momentos de asno,
tan desvalido como el propio día.

Si noche huye mi ardiente luz de día,
y por pobre olmo olvídame la rosa,
¿cómo me las veré luciendo en asno?
Que sea como fuere, ajena noche,
no huyáis del dia; ni del asno, ¡oh yegua!;
ni vos, flor, del eterno inmóvil olmo.

Mas sé bien que la rosa nunca a olmo
pertenecerá ni la noche al día,
ni un híbrido de mí querrá la yegua;

Sestina of the Unequals

A donkey am I now that watch a mare,
that morsel for a horse, not for a donkey;
then I palpate the petal of a rose
with branches, when I turn into an elm;
and all the time the firelight of my day
illuminates the pubis of the night.

From infancy I loved the secret Night
in equal measure as I did the Mare:
the Night, for being evasive of my day;
the Mare, for seeing me only as a donkey;
and not even when I am a haughty elm
can I prevail with the exquisite Rose.

How often I have dreamed I hugged the Rose!
or that I got inside the soul of Night,
yet stay I lonely, like daylight or elm,
and even as I follow the swift Mare,
whom I can never reach when I am donkey,
I am as feeble as the very day.

If Night flees from my fervid light of day,
and my poor elm is unseen by the Rose
how will I ever manage as a donkey?
But be that as it may, −O distant Night,
don't flee the Day; nor you the Donkey, Mare!
nor, Blossom, you the fixed eternal elm.

But well I know that never to an elm
will the sweet Rose belong, nor Night to day,
and no half-breed from me will please the Mare;

y solo alcanzo espinas de la rosa,
en tanto que la impenetrable noche,
me esquiva por ser día y olmo y asno.

Aunque mil atributos tengo de asno,
en mi destino pienso siendo olmo,
ante la orilla misma de la noche;
pues si fugaz mi paso cuando día,
o inmóvil punto al lado de la rosa,
que vivo y muero por la fina yegua.

¡Ay! ni olmo a la medida de la rosa,
y aun menos asno de la esquiva yegua,
mas yo dia ando siempre tras la noche.

Sextinas y otros poemas, 1970

and I shall only feel thorns in the Rose,
and always will impenetrable Night
shun me for being day and elm and donkey.

Although I have a thousand donkey-traits,
I think about my destiny, as elm
upon the very margin of the Night:
how, if my footstep fleeting is, when day,
or an immobile station near the Rose,
I live and die for the exquisite Mare.

Alas! an Elm not suited to the Rose,
Donkey, still less to the evasive Mare;
but I as Day forever chase the Night.

La cara de mis hijas

Este cielo del mundo siempre alto,
antes jamás mirado tan de cerca,
que de repente veo en el redor,
en una y otra de mis ambas hijas,
cuando perdidas ya las esperanzas
que alguna vez al fin brillara acá
una mínima luz del firmamento,
lo oscuro en mil centellas desatando;
que en cambio veo ahora por doquier,
a diario a tutiplén enceguciéndome
todo aquello que ajeno yo creía,
y en paz quedo conmigo y con el mundo
por mirar ese lustre inalcanzable,
aunque sea en la cara de mis hijas.

En alabanza del bolo alimenticio, 1979

The Face of My Daughters

This sky of the world, forever high,
not ever seen from so nearby,
is suddenly something that I see
in either daughter next to me,
long after all my hopes were lost
that perhaps suddenly at last
the firmament with a tiniest spark
might sparkle and unlock the dark.
And daily here in the surrounding
I see it blinding and abounding,
what I had thought was alien,
and find peace with myself and men
from seeing that once distant grace,
though it be in my daughter's face.

Boda de la pluma y la letra

En el gabinete del gran más allá,
apenas llegando trazar de inmediato
la elegante áurea letra codiciada,
aunque como acá nuevamente en vano,
      o bien al contrario,
que por ser allá nunca más esquiva.

En el cielo o infierno sea escrita aquella
que desdeñar suele a la pluma negra,
quien en vida acá por más que se empeñe
ni una vez siquiera escribirla puede,
      como blanca pluma,
por entre las aguas, los aires y el fuego.

Esa pluma y letra, antípodas ambas
en el horizonte del mundo terreno,
que sumo calígrafo a la áurea guarda
para el venturoso no de búho vástago,
      mas de cisne sí,
que con ella ayunte del alba a la noche.

Aunque en más allá y con otra mano,
trazar en los cuatro puntos cardinales
letrica montés, aérea y acuática,
conquistando el mundo de un plumazo solo,
      y así poderoso
más que hijo de cisne de la prenda dueño.

Wedding of the Pen and the Letter

Scarcely arrived inside the cabinet
of the Beyond, immediately to trace
the elegant, the golden, longed-for letter,
although beyond as here, again in vain—
    or even the reverse! —
her being less elusive there than ever.

In heaven or in hell let her be written,
who always so disdains the inky pen,
which here in life, being black, the more it toils,
the less is able even once to write her
    as a white feather would,
amid the waters, breezes, and the fire.

That pen and letter, so antipodal
on the horizon of the terrene world!
since the supreme calligrapher reserves her
so that some lucky sprout not of an owl,
    ah, no—but of a swan
may couple with her from sunrise to night.

Though only there, and with another hand,
to trace in all four compass-points the dear
letter, that lives in mountains, water, breeze;
thus conquering the whole world by a penstroke;
    more powerful than even
the son of a swan; the owner of the treasure.

Aquella que nunca escribir se pudo
por los crudos duelos de terrena vida,
feliz estamparla en el más allá
con un trazo dulce, suave y aromático,
        por siglos y siglos,
y en medio del ocio acá inalcanzable.

Allá en el arcano trazar una letra,
y tal olmo y hiedra con ella enlazarse,
dos esposos nuevos muy frenéticamente,
en la nupcial cámara ya no frigorífica,
        y la áurea letra
escribirla al fin con la pluma negra.

En alabanza del bolo alimenticio, 1979

The letter that could never once be written,
because of the cruel griefs of terrene life—
to stamp her happily there in the beyond,
with a sweet, smooth, and aromatic stroke,
            for ages after ages
in a deep leisure here unreachable.

There, deep in the arcane, to trace a letter,
and with her intertwine, like elm and ivy,
a newly wedded pair, deliriously,
in the no longer chilly bridal chamber;
            and the all-golden letter,
oh, at long last to write with a black pen.

Mi victoria
[*1967*]

El cielo, el monte, el mar
en pez, en piedra, en ave nos tenían
cuán separadamente
y éramos cada cual
del uno al otro como día y noche.

Y en el orbe no solo
en lontananza fuimos mal mi grado,
sino que éramos tal
en el materno claustro,
aun antes de los cierzos y los notos.

Mas aunque lejos siempre,
una vez solo verte yo soñaba,
cual áureo girasol
o desalada cebra,
que en la noche surgiera por ensalmo.

Y por fortuna fue
no vana la porfiada y dura espera,
y al cabo apareciste
en dilatada imagen
al humano linaje sobrepasando.

Porque en fin divisarte
ya girasol, ya cebra, ya señora,
victoria será mía,
que a otro nada pasma,
mas para mí lo es todo hasta la muerte.

El buen mudar, 1987

My Victory
[1967]

The sky, the mountain, sea
as fish, as stone, as bird were holding us
how wholly separate
and always we were each
unto the other as the night to day.

Not only on the orb
against my will we two were in remoteness,
but we were also so
in the maternal cloister,
even before the North Wind and the South Wind.

Yet though forever distant
only one time I dreamed of seeing you,
as of a golden sunflower
or of a nimble zebra,
that in the night arises by enchantment.

And by good luck it was
no emptiness, that hard and stubborn hope,
and you appeared at last
in a dilated image
that overtopped all human lineage.

Since at last to descry you
now sunflower, now a zebra, now a lady
will be my victory
that does not dumbfound others
but till my death for me is everything.

Las migajuelas del Rey Sumerio

El abreviado mundo de las migas
surge en la mesa al cabo de la cena
como un espejo puntualmente fiel
de las oscuras cosas apartadas,
cuando el rey de Sumeria por hartazgo
ya deja lo que nada le provoca
tras engullir la masa sacrosanta
milenio por milenio brutalmente
desde la luz de la primera aurora;
mas yo recojo raudo
mil trocitos mañana, tarde, noche,
y ceno en el ocaso a cada rato
reparadoras sobras que me mudan
tal si a nacer volviera
ahora satisfecho en cuerpo y alma.

El trigo de los prados de Sumeria,
que inalcanzable ayer entre las nubes,
de improviso hoy tocado por mis dedos
siquiera en la corteza de un mendrugo,
que el varón soberano va olvidando
sin saber que los restos en sí tienen
el mayor fruto del florido huerto
trocado por entero en blanca harina,
que a su vez se concentra en una pizca,
oculto punto allí
dentro del alimento apetecido,
que la brevedad de la pobre miga
por una gracia de los santos cielos
custodia no es de sobras,
mas de primicias sí (que yo doy fe).

56

The Crumbs of the Sumerian King

The world abbreviated of the crumbs
at dinner's end arises on the table
as if a punctual and faithful mirror
of all unnoticed isolated things,
when from satiety the Sumerian King
disdains already what in no way tempts him
since he has gobbled consecrated dough
millennium on millennium brutally
from the primeval light of the first dawn;
    but quickly I snatch up
a thousand crumblets morning, noon and night,
and in the sunset every second sup
on the refreshing leavings, that remake me
    as if I were reborn
now satisfied in body and in soul.

The barley of the meadows of Sumeria,
unreachable yesterday amid the clouds,
is suddenly today touched by my fingers,
even if only in a beggar's crust
that the male sovereign goes on forgetting
from ignorance that these leftovers contain
the greatest fruit of all the flowering orchard
entirely converted to white flour,
that is distilled still further to a crumb,
    to a recondite point
inside the nutriment so coveted;
for the brevity of a humble crumb,
by a grace given by the sacred sky,
    is monstrance not of leavings
no– rather of first fruits, as I attest.

La vergüenza ardiendo entre la cara
por comer tantas pizcas poderosas
dejadas por el comensal sumerio,
que a maravilla fueron amasadas
en el centro del más elevado horno,
tan lejos de mi mano y de mi boca;
y aunque restos caídos sobre el suelo
bien dispuestos por dentro y fuera son,
que así recuerdan la matriz celeste
en donde las primeras
causas quedaron para siempre hechas,
pues estas reflejadas allí están
en cada rico trozo espléndidamente,
que siendo flor de harina
el hambre eterno desde acá me sacia.

He aquí qué de partículas perfectas
sobre el mantel al término del día,
como pétalos en el césped sueltos,
aunque una a una cuán despedazadas
desde inmemorial tiempo sin cesar
por el supremo comensal del reino,
como un león mordiendo noche a noche

la corteza del pan inmaculado,
que al alborear harto queda entonces;
mas yo feliz recojo
de la mesa las sobras desechadas,
que saboreo como las entrañas
del óptimo potaje de la historia,
ayer de mí qué esquivo
y en virtud de los cielos hoy ya no.

Into the face there creeps a burning shame
for eating so many powerful crumblets
left here by the Sumerian commensal,
and kneaded most amazingly as if
midway in the most elevated oven,
so distant from my hand or from my mouth;
and, though but remnants fallen on the floor,
are well positioned, inside and outside,
and thus remember the celestial womb
    wherein the earliest
prime causes stayed, created once forever:
each one of which is yet reflected there,
in every tasty fragment splendidly;
    and for this Flower of Flour
herefrom eternal hunger satiates me.

There are so many and so perfect piece-lings,
here on the tablecloth at close of day,
like petals loosely scattered on the sod,
albeit how pulled to pieces one by one
from immemorial time without a pause
by the supreme Commensal of the kingdom,
who like a lion gnaws night after night
the outer crust of bread immaculate,
and stays, thereafter, stuffed, until the daybreak;

    but happily I gather
from off the table his rejected leavings,
and savor them, as though they were the heart
of the most tasty stew in history,
    shy of me yesterday,
but thanks to Heaven's favor, not today.

El sabor me lo adueño totalmente
del dulce pan jamás probado antes,
y si bien microscópicos pedazos
sin duda migas cuánto robustísimas
todas ídolo de sabrosa harina
por quien el don del gusto prevalece
desde el primer bocado terrenal,
y no otra cosa sino el gran deseo
de cenar acá y en el más allá;
que delante de mi
veo el recién venido pan sumerio,
cuya especial hechura pasa a ser
la hechura de mi bolo alimenticio
cuando saciado yazgo
por estas sobrias sobras que soñé.

Que ni un instante vuelva atrás la vida,
ni menos tú, Canción mia, otra vez
clamando por los restos;
y aunque muy tarde los devore hambriento,
temprano yo diviso
ahora el Edén al comer por fin
migajuela de migajuela. Amén.

El buen mudar, 1987

Wholly the flavor overmasters me
of a sweet bread I never tried before
and though (it's true) but microscopic pieces
they are without doubt the robustest crumbs,
the virtual idol of the fragrant flour
for which the gift of earthly taste exists
beginning with the first terrestrial bite,
and nothing other than the very need
of dining here and up in the Beyond.
    And there in front of me
I see the lately-come Sumerian bread,
of which the especial shaping comes to be
the baking of my nutrimental cud,
    when I lie satiated
by these the sober scraps that I have sung.

And not one instant let my life turn back,
and still less you, my Song, who once again
    cry out for the remains;
and though I wolf them hungrily very late,
    I can divine much sooner
where Eden is, as I partake at last
of tiny crumb on tiny crumb. Amen.

El buen mudar

El horizonte es tan inescrutable,
y no sé qué se anida tras su línea,
ni dónde empieza ni por dónde acaba,
si abajo cerca del terrenal suelo
a lo largo de una llanura verde,
o allá arriba en el alto cielo azul,
que deseo mudarme
a un punto de la línea horizontal
y a buen recaudo allí
ponerme para siempre por entero,
porque desde la cuna
tal lugar lo he buscado con porfía
más allá de la luz y las tinieblas.

Nunca diviso ni uno de sus limites,
que seguro posee un par de alas
como pájaro o ángel de la guarda,
y se va el horizonte así volando
no sé si a otro término del mundo
o hacia un ángulo del empíreo hermético,
que el lugar codiciado
huidizo e inalcanzable es dia a dia,
paraje oculto aun,
pero no dejo nunca de buscarlo
hoy despierto o durmiendo,
mañana navegando en el Leteo,
que allí a perpetuidad deseo estar.

The Good Change

The horizon is so far, inscrutable,
nor do I know what nests behind its line,
nor what it rises from, nor where it ends,
if underneath, close to the terrene soil,
contiguous with a long, verdant prairie,
or upwards, yonder in deep azure sky,
    I long to change myself
into a point of the horizon-line,
    there in safe custody
to put myself forever and completely,
    since from the very cradle
stubbornly I have searched for such a place
that is beyond the light, beyond the darkness.

I never can descry one of its limits,
and certainly it has a pair of wings,
and like a bird, or like a guardian angel,
the whole horizon thus departing flies
I know not if to another end of the world
or towards a nook of the arcane empyrean;
    and that place, coveted
day after day, is fleet and unapproachable,
    a spot till now arcane,
though I can never cease from seeking it
    today asleep or waking,
tomorrow navigating in the Lethe,
and there in perpetuity long to be.

Espero que aparezca de repente,
aunque sea un puntito imperceptible,
para enrumbar los pasos ayer ciegos,
donde disfrute la futura edad,
tal nave que de popa a proa arrimase
a tierra firme tras feroz tormenta;
y basta un solo átomo
del remoto paraje aún no visto,
que si lo veo al fin,
en pos de él pronto vuelo, nado y ando,
que a la vez sea tal
la mudanza hacia el escogido sitio,
en el que yo administre todo mi ocio.

Que dada la ocasión de vivir hoy,
en el terrenal mundo todavía,
me encamino animoso sin cautela
a la vivienda natural y segura
no cerca de la humana prisión negra,
y menos de la inoportuna muerte,
pues he aquí la morada:
visible punto en la horizontal línea
para alcanzar ahora
lo que fue escatimado en primavera
en la pasada edad,
que justo premio es hoy el buen mudar,
y rindo eternas gracias que así sea.

17 de diciembre de 1986

El buen mudar, 1987

I hope that it may suddenly appear,
although it be a pointlet, imperceptible,
to orient footsteps that had been blind,
a place where I enjoy the age to come,
like a ship poop-to-prow in the protection
of *terra firma* after a fierce storm;
    and one atom suffices
of that remoteness even if not seen
    and if at last I see it,
behind it quickly I fly and swim and walk,
    so as to feel an instant
removal towards the choicest site, wherein
alone I may administer my leisure.

And given the occasion to live today
although as yet in the sublunary world,
I take the road with courage, without cunning,
toward a good lodging, natural and safe,
and never near the pitch-black human prison,
and even less, death that comes inopportune,
    since my abode is that
point visible on the horizon-line;
    so as to reach at last
what stingily was given in the springtime
    of that age that has passed;
and the right prize today is this good change
for which I give eternal gratitude.

December 17, 1986

El nido codiciado

Es el buen mudar irse a otro mundo
en donde arda la llama del amor,
que locura sería no buscar
la mínima señal del punto aquel
como una estrella en la noche oscura,
que el caudal de su luz es generosa
con quien busca el lugar con gran porfía
para marcharse allí como si fuera
el altísimo reino anticipado,
pues la línea del horizonte escarba
con las filudas garras de un dragón,
que en pajarillo cambia de repente
al encontrar el nido codiciado,
en cuyo seno basta para siempre
un par de migas y una leve paja.

28 de diciembre de 1986

El buen mudar, 1987

The Coveted Nest

The good move is to go to another world
within which burns the fire that is our love
and madness would be not to search for even
the tiniest signal twinkling from that point
as in dark night a star. And so from thence
light overflowing searches from afar
what stubborn heart soever seeks it out
and travels thither, as if soon to enter
that so high up, so long-awaited kingdom.
And clawing at the line of the horizon
he claws with the sharp talons of a dragon
that suddenly turns into the tiny bird
that recognized the nest which it had longed for,
in whose warm bosom just a pair of crumbs
and a light airy straw suffice forever.

December 28, 1986

No salir jamás

¿Cuándo, cuándo de nuevo volveré,
en qué minuto, día, año o centuria,
al sacro rinconcillo de mi dueña,
paraje oculto para mí guardado,
y a merced de su excelsa carne allí
yacer adentro y no salir jamás?
A aquel lugar yo quiero retornar,
hasta el punto central eternamente,
introducido en el secreto valle,
y en ella cuerpo y alma así cuajado.
No quiero nada más sino volver
adonde fugazmente ayer estuve,
cruzar el umbral con seguro paso
y ahora para siempre allí quedarme,
no como dueño de un terrenal sitio,
mas por entero rey del universo.

4 de enero de 1986

Bajo el sol de la medianoche rojo, 1990

Never to go out any more

When, when will I return again? In what
minute, or day, or year, or century,
to a sweet sacred corner of my mistress,
the occult nook reserved for me alone,
and so by grace of her irradiant flesh
to lie indoors and never more go out?
And to that place I want, O, to return,
eternally into its central point;
and introduced into her secret valley,
wherein soul and body come together.
Now I want nothing more: just to return
to where I was so fleetingly; I want
to cross the threshold with a secure footstep
and in that selfsame place remain forever,
not as the owner of a piece of earth
but as the king of all the universe.

Las cosas de la casa

He aquí al fin la casa bien oculta
tras las nubes de la celeste bóveda,
preservándola de los fieros cacos
terrenales que alrededor acechan;
y así poder vivir metido en ella
en medio de una tibia paz siquiera,
aferrándose a las calladas cosas
que no dejan de estar a cada rato
acompañando como dulces seres;
porque al paso del día y de la noche
todo aquello que inerte y fiel yace
en las proximidades de uno siempre,
en el templado seno de la casa,
resulta parte de la invisible alma,
ya una sola naturaleza exacta.

Acción de gracias, 1992

The Things of the House

Here is the house, well hidden
behind the clouds of the celestial vault,
protecting it from the ferocious thieves
of earth, who lie in ambush all around it;
thus to be able to live snug inside it
amidst at any rate a tepid peace
so tightly clinging to the quiet things
that never for one instant cease to be
sweet creatures that accompany a soul;
since with the passage of the day and night
all this that so inert and faithful lies
nearby, in one's proximity, forever
within the temperate bosom of the house,
turns out to be part of one's unseen soul,
made now into a single, exact nature.

Recuerdo de hermano

Al fin he descubierto palmo a palmo
cómo es la superficie de tus días,
y he debido cruzar osadamente
las montañas ceñidas por las nubes
y espumosos océanos que braman,
hasta llegar al punto
del cual tú nada sabes,
aunque allí tus espirituales huellas
diviso y palpo en todos los confines,
donde nunca has estado ni un instante.

Ni de las moscas los zumbidos leves
cuando solo te quedas de improviso
al salir cada cual afuera rápido
a hacer las cosas de la vida diaria,
contentos porque así de ti se alejan;
que tal falta de ruido
acá también se siente,
y es ese gran silencio que aparece
anidándose en los alrededores
como si en vez de mí estuvieras tú.

Esos muros, el piso y el vacío
son como cosas corporales tuyas,
que en ti se han extendido hasta formar
contigo y con el cuarto un bulto único
todo de cal, arena, carne y alma;
y cómo por completo
reedificado ha sido
en lo remoto en que me encuentro hoy,
y allí dándome cuenta mido al fin
tu cuadrado, tu círculo, tu mundo.

Memory of My Brother

At last I have discovered inch by inch
how is the superficies of your days,
for I have had to travel, daring all,
over the mountains girdled by the clouds
and over foaming and resounding oceans,
   so as to reach the point
   of which you nothing know
except that there your spiritual traces
I sight or palpate on every horizon,
where you have never for one instant been.

Not even the light buzzing of the flies
whenever, suddenly, you are alone
since everyone has quickly gone outside
to do the little things of daily life,
glad that that way they move away from you;
   and such absence of noise
   in this place, too, is felt
and is an immense silence that appears
in the surroundings and there makes its nest
as if instead of me it were you here.

Those walls, the floor, with all their emptiness
are like corporeal things of yours,
that have stretched into you, so as to form
from you and from the room a unique bundle
made out of lime and sand and flesh and soul;
   as if it had been wholly
   once vanished reconstructed
in the remoteness where I am today,
in which I take the measurements at last
of your pure square, pure circle, purest world.

Aunque así sea ingreso en esta réplica
de tu cuarto en un pardo sitio acá,
donde soy como clavo en la madera,
inmóvil, solitario exactamente
como tú en tu mismísimo recinto,
cuyo umbral no traspaso
e igual como los otros
allá de ti me aparto muy temprano,
y arrinconado quedas en un ángulo;
(pero acá está en mí reproducido).

Pues nunca más te vuelvo las espaldas
y como en el pasado ambos estamos
en la cuna, en el cuarto, en la morada
bajo los dulces ojos maternales,
tal ligados por una fibra idéntica;
y la esfera fatal
y la esfera feliz
(la tuya y la mía) se unen y es la casa
de papá y mamá, en cuya compañía
de nuevo como ayer, y así por siempre.

Acción de gracias, 1992

Though only thus I enter this replica
of your apartment in a drab location
where now I like a nail am in the wood,
and motionless, alone, must be exactly
like you inside your space, your very own,
   whose sill I do not cross
   but as the others did
I leave you very early and depart,
and you remain there, cornered, in an angle
(except that here you are reproduced in me).

For never again do I turn my back on you,
and even as in the past, so now both of us
are in the crib, the room, the dwelling-place
beneath the sweet eyes of our mother, tied
there tightly by a thread identical
   and the fate-heavy sphere
   and the felicitous
(your own, and mine) unite; it is the house
of Papa and Mama, in whose company,
as yesterday, so now, and so forever.

¡Salve, Spes!

*(Personificación romana de la Esperanza,
a quien vislumbro a través de un devoto suyo
que vivió en la era cristiana)*

Allá en el horizonte apareciendo
como el sol de la medianoche rojo
cuyos rayos irradian por doquier,
que exactamente es esta la Esperanza
en la gastada edad de Eva y Adán,
y a cada rato los sentidos puestos
profundamente en ella
por ser el absoluto norte ahora
atrayendo los pasos
automáticamente ya por siempre.

Es vivir aferrándose a la creencia
de coronar lo que se quiere tanto,
nada más que el inmaculado pan
para engullirlo sin dejar migaja
con la más voraz gula (que es la anímica)
como la res comiendo el rico pasto;
y es esta la mejor
manera para hacer frente a la Parca,
como que satisfecho
de un buen vivir se pase al buen morir.

No hay mayor caudal ni mayor sapiencia
que estar sujeto al cabo de los años
a la suprema idea con fijeza
de haber en este mundo o en el otro
la felicidad que es inalcanzable

Salve, Spes!

*(Roman personification of Hope
glimpsed through one of her devotees
who lived in the Christian era)*

Yonder appearing out on the horizon,
like the red sun of midnight, the red sun
the rays of which irradiate everywhere.
For Hope is this exactly for the creatures
of the exhausted age of Eve and Adam,
with all our senses every second fixed
   profoundly onto her
for being now the absolutest North
   attracting our footsteps
already automatically forever.

It is to live tied tight to a belief
that one can crown what has been coveted,
immaculate pure bread and nothing more,
so as to gobble it to the last crumb
with fiercest gluttony (that of the soul),
like head of livestock eating richest fodder;
   and this is the best way
of meeting with a Parca face to face,
   as if thus satisfied
from living well one passed to dying well.

There is no greater wealth nor greater wisdom
than at the end of life to be subjected
so fixedly to the supreme idea
of having in this world or in the other
the happiness that is unattainable

por ser desconocida enteramente,
y aunque en estado informe
uno de figurársela no cesa
igual que una deidad
recóndita, qué importa, mas benigna.

Y encontrarse en el agua, fuego y aire
en las postrimerías propagado,
preparándose a alcanzar por último
lo tanto deseado cuando mozo
que por entonces era cada cosa
no pequeña sino nonata pizca
al pie del atroz cero,
aunque hoy en cambio cuántas ilusiones
y así esperando el todo
con igual brío ayer la ciega nada.

Es el sol de la medianoche rojo
que ha llegado el momento que relumbre,
y al fin no ya el mal ceño de los días
que era fatal presagio inexorable
tal si los nuevos años semejaran
tejido de tinieblas harto espesas;
que repentinamente
acá la esencia del nocturno sol
de la bóveda arriba,
y la oscuridad queda disipada.

Hoy el desconocido sentimiento
entre alegría y pasmo cómo bulle,
que ayer se le ignoraba día y noche
porque la dilatada edad delante
de fijo disuadía imaginarlo

because it is so utterly unknown;
    and though it still is shapeless
one never ceases picturing it to oneself
    as equal to a goddess,
arcane (what does it matter?) but benignant.

To find oneself in water, fire and air
being propagated at the end of life,
preparing ultimately to attain
what as a boy one so acutely longed for,
which at the time was every single thing,
not small, but unborn, tiny, at the foot
    of the atrocious zero,
although today in turn what great illusions!
    and thus await the All
as yesterday one did blind Nothingness.

It is the sun of midnight, a red sun
whose moment has arrived; now it can shine—
dispel at last that evil ring of days,
that was a deadly omen never prayed to,
as if the new years always seemed to be
too thickly wholly woven out of darkness;
    for lo! now suddenly
here is the essence of the nocturnal sun
    of the celestial vault
and the first darkness now stays dissipated.

Today that unknown sentiment between
deep happiness and wonder, how it stirs,
that day and night was yesterday unknown,
because the spacious age that lay before it
dissuaded one from any image of it,

como si nunca necesario fuera,
mas todo cambia ahora
en el sublunar globo en que se nace,
y he aquí el tiempo próximo
que los dedos vivientes cogen fuertes.

Eso que ayer jamás ni un pedacito
palpar se pudo de la gran fortuna
como aquellos dichosos qué campantes
de acá para acullá seguros iban;
aunque para quien en ayunas vive
a la postre tal como hoy lo descubre
le fue cuán adecuado
que por ansioso no como los otros
la ley divina aprende
al esperar el cielo desde el suelo.

Pues aplaca la gula en el otoño,
y no le importa haber vivido al margen
de la dorada primavera entonces
sin alcanzar las flores ni las mieses
que con profusión Flora les otorga
al pastor y a la ninfa en los umbrales
de la tierna estación,
que las dádivas son mejores cuando
el paladar se torna
como nunca más fino hasta el final.

Allá entre dos exequias flaco estuvo
cada decena de años puntualmente
sin atesorar la menor idea
de un futuro existir halagador,

as if it were not, ever, necessary;
   but everything is changing
in the sublunar globe where births occur,
   and here is the finale
that living fingers fiercely fasten on.

What yesterday was never, not one jot,
able to be palpated of good fortune,
when some how lucky and contentedly
used to traverse securely to and fro;
but for the one who lives by always fasting
it was at last, as he discovers now,
   for him how adequate!
and in anxiety, not like the others,
   he's learning divine law
by waiting for the heavens from the soil.

For in the autumn gluttony is appeased;
nor does it matter to have lived on the edge,
in former times, of the gold tide of springtime
unable to reach the blossoms and the wheat
that in profusion Flora promises
the shepherd and the nymph, in the beginnings
   of the most tender season,
and all that she vouchsafes is best whenever
   the palate turns more subtle,
towards the end, than it has ever been.

How feeble it was between two exequies,
each punctual new decade, all the years
that did not treasure up the least idea
of the to-come more flattering existence;

que tanto era el dolor por la partida
de quienes hoy son sus paternos ídolos;
y en verdad merced a ellos
recién ha acariciado el buen mudar,
inmediato o después,
de indiferente a archiesperanzado.

Esta inimaginable feliz suerte
reina en el fértil prado que fue siempre
invisible, impalpable o inodoro,
y helo aqui todo tan inmarchitable,
que es la porción ayer no disfrutada,
hoy alumbrando como un áureo nimbo
cuando más se requiere
justamente en las horas decisivas
a la espera de aquello
que tarde viene, mas sí llega al fin.

¡Salve, Spes!, 2000

and so immense was grief, at the departure
of those who are today paternal Manes;
   and thanks to them in truth,
recently he befriended the good change,
   immediate or later,
from an indifferent to arch-hopeful soul

This unimaginable happy luck
reigns in the fertile meadow that was always
invisible, impalpable, odorless,
and here stands still, unwitherable, all
that yesterday was a portion not enjoyed
that shines at present like a golden nimbus
   when it is needed most
exactly in the most decisive hours
   for sake of hope in that
which comes so late but comes, yes, comes at last.

IX

Sí, santos cielos, que arda para siempre
la fuerza del amor en cuerpo y alma,
dando fe que resulta inapagable
la candela de las candelas reina
que es la tea del ara que está aquí
en el centro del corazón hambriento,
porque ardoroso late
cuando Eva en el umbral apenas surge
encendiendo de súbito
las imberbes o las maduras llamas.

Ojalá que de nuevo en su interior
e igual que ayer aquel estar feliz
ya entrando y ya saliendo como autómata,
que cuanto antes volver es lo anhelado
para partir de allí hacia el más allá
conociendo la placentera vida
del mismísimo Edén
y anticipadamente disfrutándola
merced a Eva, que es todo,
aunque tengamos de ella solo partes.

Nada más que en el punto codiciado
horas, días, años o siglos previos
al último suspiro inexorable,
que breve o largo tiempo da lo mismo

IX

*A part l'adoration de Dieu, la
voluptè est donc l'act le plus
religieux de la vie.*
—MALCOLM DE CHAZAL

Yes, sacred Heaven, may it burn forever,
the force of love in body and in soul,
and prove forever inextinguishable
that candle of the candles of the queen
that is the torch that stands upon the altar
of the pure center of the hungry heart;
   for ardently it throbs
whenever on the doorsill Eve arises,
  and kindles suddenly
the young and beardless or maturer flames.

If only anew in its interior,
equal to yesterday, this happiness!
this going in, out, like automata;
for to return at once is what is longed for,
so as to leave that place for the Beyond,
once having known the pleasurable life
  of even the ancient Eden,
enjoying it in anticipation, thanks
  to Eve, who is everything,
albeit we have only pieces of her.

Oh nothing more than, in the longed-for point,
hours, days, or years, or centuries, before
the ultimate inexorable sigh,
for whether brief or long, it does not matter,

cuando son cosas de la eternidad,
que por adelantado allí gobierna
en donde se produce
la unión de la pareja en pleno otoño,
que aunque dos seres ínfimos
son rey y reina desde que se encuentran.

Y en este punto estar y nunca en otro,
como ayer por los cuatro lados bien,
que es lo que más se ansía en este mundo
entrar y salir día a día siempre,
o estar perennemente palpitando
allí a la vez en aire, fuego y agua,
y es la mejor manera
de andar acá por el restante trecho,
adelantando pues
un paso en pos de la suprema cima.

Ahora y no antes es mejor vivir
en esta situación encaminándose
con los ojos del alma y cuerpo fijos
en el próximo nuevo estar celeste,
que es oportuno conocerlo hoy
entre el gozo instantáneo postrimero
y el perdurable éxtasis
que ignoto no será por tal motivo
previéndolo asombrado
en la porción corpórea de la musa.

No salir ni una vez del lugar magno
en el cual la sensualidad gobierna
desde acá a los confines siderales,
y el ápice es allí y no en otro sitio,

when all these things are of eternity,
and out there, in advance, are governed by,
   whenever it is produced,
the full autumnal union of the couple
   who though the humblest beings
are king and queen the moment they have met.

And to be in that point, never in another,
as yesterday on all four sides content,
which is, what is most coveted in this world
to enter, exit, day by day forever
or to be quivering perennially
at the same time in air and fire and water,
   and that is the best way
on earth of walking the remaining distance,
   advancing steadily
one step below the highest height of all.

Today and not before, it is well to live
in the position of a traveller,
with the soul's eyes, the body's eyes both fixed
upon a new and near celestial state,
and opportune to recognize it now,
between the final instantaneous joy
   and lasting ecstasy,
nor will it be unknown for such a motive
   foreseeing it astonished
in the corporeal portion of the Muse.

And never once to leave the glorious place,
in which our sensuality rules and reaches
from here unto the boundaries of the stars,
and there the apex is and nowhere else,

y donde empieza la ascensión directa
a coronar un ser indivisible,
como la vid y el olmo
o perro y perra unidos cien mil horas,
que lo sublime humano
alza al cielo la boda en este suelo.

Y entretejerse entrambos hilo a hilo
como compacta urdimbre y homogénea
y es el mudar perfecto día y noche
en una sola carne y esqueleto,
y en una sola el alma de los dos,
que es el todo sin par apetecido
en un único pálpito
como si en esta unión ambos dejaran
de ser dos codo a codo,
y en cambio exactamente eterno uno.

Otra vez estar arropado acá
entre la carnal envoltura amada,
y así la abolición de la pareja
que no volverá a ser en adelante
dos amantes a la intemperie fríos
mirándose o hablándose de lejos,
y nunca más entonces
como la plata y oro frente a frente
en los ignotos límites,
que un solo ser qué de quilates vale.

Es el alto tabernáculo al fin
ese monte de Venus codiciado
donde guardar el pasmo compartido
bajo la forma del resplandor rojo

and where direct ascension has begun
to crown a creature indivisible,
    as vine clings to the elm
or hound and bitch do, for ten thousand hours,
    and the sublimely human
lifts to the sky our wedding on this soil.

And thread by thread to intertwine ourselves
like a homogenous and compact warp,
and is the perfect change by day and night
into one single skeleton and flesh
uniting in one soul the souls of both,
which is the peerless all, that is desired
    in but one unique throbbing
as if in union both of us desisted
    from being elbow to elbow
and two changed to exactly eternal one.

Once more to be wrapped up
inside the beloved carnal covering
and thus the abolition of the couple
that in the future will no longer be
two lovers in rough weather outdoors, cold,
watching each other or talking from afar
    and thenceforth never more
like silver next to gold brow unto brow,
    on some unknown frontier;
so truly precious is a single being

It is the high tabernacle in the end
this mount of Venus so long coveted
whereon to keep the shared astonishment
beneath the form of the red splendor

de la primera aurora de la Tierra
brillando sobre Adán y Eva muy juntos,
uno en el otro dentro
ceñidos por la aureola luminosa,
que muda el tabernáculo
en la casa del éxtasis celeste.

Todo empieza con la sensualidad
no del reino del bolo alimenticio,
ni tampoco de las sensibles artes,
sino aquella latiendo en las alturas
del alma y de la carne puntualmente,
sobrepujando el tiempo y el espacio,
y donde se entrelazan
el tacto, vista, olfato, oído y gusto,
como si los sentidos
de cada dama y hombre allí se unieran.

¡Salve, Spes!, 2000

of the first aurora of the Earth
shining on Adam and Eve, so closely joined,
   the one inside the other
girdled by the luminous aureola
   that changes the tabernacle
into the house of a celestial ecstasy.

All starts here with a sensuality
not governed by the alimentary bolus
and not from the kingdom of the sensuous arts
but one which throbs upon the very heights
of the soul and of the body punctually
so overtopping all of time and space,
   and wherein intertwine
our touch and sight and smell and taste and hearing,
   as if the various senses
of every man and woman there united.

Al pintor Giovanni Donato da Montorfano
(*1440-1510*)

Yaces sin gozar el favor de nadie,
y es tu soledad tanta un claro espejo
de aquello que sucede exactamente
ayer, hoy y mañana cuando todos
te tornan de improviso las espaldas,
como el mayor efecto del olvido;
que este sombrío estado
demuestra en qué terminan finalmente
el físico vigor y el sabio seso
empeñados a fondo
en hacer bien las cosas del vivir,
que al final tal esfuerzo sobrehumano
resulta empresa de pequeña hormiga.

No te escabulles de tu mala estrella
y en cambio inmóvil hora a hora pasas
padeciendo cuán resignadamente
el desdén de los fieles de Leonardo,
que discurren delante sin mirar
ni siquiera de reojo el fruto sumo
de tus cien mil desvelos
cuando pusiste lo mejor de ti
en homenaje a El Crucificado,
vasta pintura tuya
que no la pueden doblegar las guerras
ni la del tiempo que puntual destruye
ni menos la lid de los hombres fieros.

To the Painter Giovanni Donato da Montorfano
(1440-1510)

Not knowing the favor of anyone you lie;
your so great solitude is a bright mirror
of what forever punctually happens
(the other day, today, again tomorrow)
when suddenly all turn their backs on you
like an effect, the greatest, of oblivion;
   and this obscure estate
well demonstrates what finally awaits
physical vigor and the knowing brain
   when either has been pawned
in doing well what one must do to live
till at the end such superhuman effort
we see is the enterprise of a little ant.

You never escape from your unlucky star,
and as a result immobile, hour on hour,
you pass in suffering how resignedly,
disdained by Leonardo's faithful flock,
that flows before you, to and fro, not looking
(not even glancingly) at the ripe fruit
   of your ten thousand toils,
when you put everything that was best in you
in simple homage to The Crucified,
   your immense painting
that no mere wars can ever cause to bend
nor even Time that punctually topples,
nor even the contention of fierce men.

Mas pese a tu paleta y tu pincel,
has terminado siendo un émulo
del varón y la dama desdeñados
por quienes ellos aman día a día
que exactamente así te encuentras tú
al sufrir los desaires de las gentes,
y en verdad mucho más
que el amante transido en su dolor
en el espacio de una corta vida,
y en cambio siglo a siglo
percibiendo tú en el mayor silencio
que ni la menor atención te prestan
cuando huyéndote pasan sin mirarte.

Y adviertes más que todos lo que ocurre
en tus alrededores diariamente
aunque no puedes preservarte nunca
de la gélida indiferencia en torno
dictada por el hado inexorable
ordenando que víctima tú seas
como un manso cordero
bajo el esquivo gesto incomprensible
de tantos que muy cerca de ti cruzan;
mas es hiel que no mancha
el alma de la que soberano eres,
fábrica de tu incolúmne pintura
por encima de los siglos firme y fresca.

Eres el sumo inadvertido ser
sin parangón en todo el pardo mundo,
a quien a cada rato lo soslayan
como si así te hubiera sucedido
desde la cuna puntualmente siempre,

But notwithstanding your palette and brush,
you ended this way, as though emulating
a gentleman or gentle girl disdained
by someone whom they love day after day,
and this exactly is how you find yourself,
on suffering the snubs of everyone;
    or actually much more
than would a lover broken by his pain
in the brief space of an exhausted life
    as century after century
you notice in the ever greater silence,
that people pay you not the least attention
as, fleeing you, they pass by without looking.

You notice more than anyone what happens
in your surroundings daily, every hour,
although you never can protect yourself
from the ice-like indifference around you,
dictated by a Fate inexorably
ordaining that you be as much a victim
    as was the gentle lamb,
beneath the incomprehensible quick gesture
made by so many passing by so near you;
    but such gall cannot stain
the soul which you are the sovereign master:
the manufacture of an unscathed painting
so firm and fresh atop the centuries.

You are supremest of unnoticed creatures,
without comparison, in the whole drab world,
whom every single second they avoid,
as if this had been happening to you
from cradle onward punctually forever:

en donde ayer sin mimos de tus padres
que su cariño daban
a tu hermano mayor enteramente;
que nunca en nada fuiste primogénito
y resignado vives
en estado dispar tu eternidad,
arriba en las empíreas salas árbitro,
abajo donde nadie en ti repara.

En las hospitalarias estrofas, 2002

without caresses yesterday, when your parents
   were giving their affection
already wholly to your elder brother;
you who were not first-born in anything
   and live, in the acceptance
of that unlike state, your eternity,
above in the empyreal palace umpire,
below where no one stops to look at you.

Cavilación del caminante

A la memoria de Paul W. Borgeson, Jr.

Diariamente camino siempre
por la faz del sublunar mundo
para preservar la salud,
y de preferencia en un parque
donde plantas y animalillos
viven codo con codo en paz;
y por allí feliz discurro
sin reparar que a unos seres,
justo como yo en plena vida,
involuntariamente piso.

Y a la verdad qué bien estoy,
aunque rápido asesinándolos
a quienes acá abajo yacen
a rastras entre suelo y cielo
sin poder esquivar la muerte
que les llega así de improviso
cuando alguien viene en dos zancadas
y con la suela del zapato
sin más ni más así deshace
cada mínimo hijo de Dios.

He aquí la multitud de hormigas
que dan el suspiro postrero
a causa de las mil pisadas
del caminante cotidiano
en homicida convertido,
no queriéndolo, no, sin duda;

The Walker's Perplexity

To the memory of Paul W. Borgeson, Jr.

I always take a daily walk
upon the face of the sublunar
world so as to preserve my health,
and preferably in a park,
where plants and tiny animals
are living side by side in peace;
and thither I stroll happily
not noticing that on some creatures
that are as full of life as I
involuntarily I step.

To tell the truth, how fit I feel,
although I swiftly assassinate
whatever lives lie underneath
me in between the earth and sky,
things powerless to dodge a death
that comes upon them unforeseen
if some late-comer in two strides
and with the footsole of his shoe,
without the smallest fuss, destroys
every too tiny son of God.

Here is the multitude of ants
that must surrender their last breath
by reason of the thousand steps
of someone on his daily walk
converted into a murderer,
against his will, yes, without doubt;

mas tales son las circunstancias
en que un gigante humano mata
al animalillo invisible
e inerme ante el andar ajeno.

Es el más inextinguible hecho,
y por añadidura absurdo,
que alguien por preservarse a fondo
—¡tal como yo cada mañana!—
de un tajo la vida le siegue
a aquel que nunca daña a nadie
ni a los imperceptibles seres;
que el firmamento entonces caiga,
igual que un castillo de naipes,
sobre mí un mal día. Así sea.

El alternado paso de los hados, 2006

but such the circumstances are
when a gigantic human kills
a tiny, unseen animal
that cannot fight the alien footstep.

It is so irreversible
and even, I would say, absurd
that someone trying to stay healthy—
as I do! each and every morning—
with one stroke slashes life from someone
who did no harm to other creatures,
not even those invisible;
so may the firmament collapse
exactly like a house of cards
on me, some evil day. So be it.

Cuando los estorbos se van

No solo la noche cuán inexorable,
sino por igual un acoso fiero
de estorbos pesados, que justo fue así
en la primavera del distante ayer
   cuando asiduo andaba
del reino interior a la blanca página.

He allí a la sazón los impedimentos
de la más variada índole en el mundo,
por causa excesiva del humano numen
que sin proponérselo desataba a diario
   en sueño y vigilia
aparentemente contra el buen vivir.

Pero de improviso he aquí el áureo mudar
de las circunstancias cuánto negativas,
que de arriba abajo obra por fortuna,
y la oscura noche pasa a ser aurora
   en medio del pasmo
de aquel que creía en tinieblas todo.

Y llegó el otoño y las circunstancias
de la boda atávica desta pluma y letra
cuán desemejantes resultan entonces
pues hoy me aproximan a lejana dama
   y al don terrenal
de leer por siempre (aunque mal que bien).

When the Obstacles Vanish

Not only such inexorable night
but, equally, ferocious persecution
by heavy obstacles, that were exactly
thus in my springtime, distant yesterday,
   when I walked constantly
from my interior realm to the blank page.

There were at that time such impediments,
of the most varied nature in the world,
by the exclusive cause of human will
that unawares were constantly unleashed
   daily in dream, in waking,
apparently against my living well.

But suddenly the golden permutation
of circumstances so far negative
that works by fortune from the top to bottom:
and the dark night has brightened into dawn
   amid the stupefaction
of him whose faith was wholly in the darkness.

Then Autumn came, and the circumstances
of the atavistic wedding of this pen
with letters, once dissimilar, have changed;
they take me now to the once distant Lady
   and a terrestrial gift:
to read forever, though imperfectly.

Es el tiempo feliz desconocido antes
cuando ahora el numen viene acompañado
del ardoroso amor y el saber celeste,
justo un gran presente de los santos cielos,
  que es como vivir
por anticipado la eternidad próxima.

El alternado paso de los hados, 2006

It is the happy time, unknown before,
when now the Will arrives, accompanied
by fervid love and a celestial knowledge,
which is the present of the holy heavens,
    as though I lived that present
anticipating all eternity.

REFLECTIONS ON THE TRANSLATIONS

These translations from the poetry Carlos Germán Belli, were made by Karl David Maurer (September 12, 1948-May 4, 2015) over a period of thirty years, in conversation with Spanish-speaking family and friends, with me, with Karl's students, and with the encouragement of Carlos Germán Belli. The translation went slowly, unhurriedly, a sign of what Karl called his "immeasurable" love for Belli's oeuvre and all he adored in it: "one thing that I find only in him and in Mandelstam: that subtle, fine humor that reflects happiness, even when he is saying the most terrible things!"

Karl alighted on thirty-five poems from eleven of Belli's books—nearly half a century of his work—and lingered over each. "You know," he wrote me in August 2014, "a trouble with verse-translations is, one can't just sit down and grind them out. There's a bit of magic involved—or to use a less pretentious word, sheer luck—and if I lose that, the poem goes dead. I often wonder what it is. It's something like this: when the 'literal' English meaning of the Latin, or Spanish, suggests a musical and syntactic pattern, for which I happen to feel a *hunger*. If it doesn't, nothing is possible—I can't touch the poem even if it's beautiful. If it does, then I have a bit of magic to work with—but it's faint and hard to find and very easy to lose. And once lost, it tends to stay lost" (8/6/2014). He added a little later: "Every now and then some translation that seemed the *most* dismal, suddenly mutates into a very good one. That's happened to me more than once."

I saw it happen, if only from a distance. I clarified passages, offering literal versions of this line or that, or roughing out an entire poem, and Karl would respond with English verse and with gratitude —"a purer gratitude when (as often) your suggestions don't ignore the English meter." "I so hate groping in the dark, intuiting the meaning. [...] Just give me a lit. translation of any poem, or poem-cluster (either 'diachronic' or a batch from one book), and I'll make English verse. [...] I just lack the time (I'm so overworked and so tired) to spend hours with the dict. figuring out the literal meaning" (KM to CM, stealing time from his teaching at the University of Dallas and from his translation of the Latin poetry of Jacob Balde.) What I took to be the "literal" meaning sometimes disappointed him. "Thanks hugely [...] But good God, what bad luck that for accuracy, for the sake of truth, the translator-slave has to lose half his music (or lose at least irony) by erasing every one of these latent double meanings [...] But to a translator you have to say, 'Sorry, but truth trumps everything. If you want to write your own poem, do it, but don't call it a translation'" (KM to CM, 3/27/2015)

We read together—always by email—several drafts of each poem, puzzling over word and image. "If you ever get second or third (or fifth, or tenth) thoughts, please send them," he wrote me in August 2014, and again, two weeks before his death: "Think twice and three times, about this poem; I don't feel at all sure you're right, though I don't feel a bit sure I'm right either" (4/15/2015). Few of these translations satisfied him. This poem or that would have to stay *as is*, "with all its sins on his head"—a phrase worthy of Belli who acknowledges with a smile "el sonar discordante de la lira" ("the discordant sound of [his own] lyre." Occasionally, a line would stump the translator completely: "It's a nut I can't crack; a trout I can't catch; a riddle I can't solve" (3/30/2015). When Belli wrote Karl an encouraging email, my brother asked me to respond for him; he couldn't do so himself without talking about his translations and there were still "bad places that I can't see how to fix. And so like the fabulous Ostrich, I bury my head in the sand, and don't take it out till I feel the danger has gone away!" (2/16/15).

A computer file on his desktop contained multiple versions of each poem and, because of his premature death, no final manuscript, posing problems for his fraternal editor. I have tried to give the latest version of each poem. In a few of these poems, bearing in mind his dictum—"truth trumps everything"—I have silently emended a line or replaced a word, in order to avoid an erroneous reading.

Trusting they will interest both readers of Belli and fellow translators of poetry—those who, like Karl, try to "take hold of the form that flees" and love "the relating of language to the heart-beat and the footstep" ("that's what 'meter' really is," he wrote his daughter Mia), I offer in the notes that follow a sampling of his reflections on his own translations, which cleave to Belli's verse forms and syntax and offer a memorable image of Belli's peculiar forms of poetic speech. "I never read any line of verse, ever," Karl wrote me on 2/28/15, "without noticing the exact metrical game (and if I can find none, I take *no* interest in it; I'd rather read prose); and the same with any stanza; I can't rest till I've figured out exactly what the rules are." Another of his rules as translator: "preserve the hypotaxis… I also think that a translator should at least slightly mime the wild word order ('hyperbaton' we call it in classics) because that, too, [can be] full of charm" (KM to Mia, 1/18/2011). And indent the shorter lines, the trimeters, even when the original is arranged otherwise: "I feel that for English the indentations are needed, especially with verse that, like [Belli's], is not rhymed. For when the lines expand and contract without indentations, it looks too much like free verse" (2/20/2015).

Brotherly love has been a constant of this belated little book—whether Belli's love for his brother Alfonso or my own for Karl as older brother and friend, poet, classicist, teacher and prodigious reader and translator. In the notes that follow I have also drawn on Carlos Germán Belli, *Morar en la superficie. Prosas*, Fondo de Cultura Económica 2015, abbreviated as *Morar*) and *Los versos juntos 1946-2008. Poesía completa (VJ)*. Notes marked KM are by Karl Maurer, the rest are mine, as are translations from *Morar en la superficie*.

For help in realizing this book I am grateful to David Rade, Marianne Jankowski, to Mia, Felipe, Timothy and Holly Maurer, to Bárbara and Verónica Cortínez, to Efraín Kristal and to María Estrella Iglesias.

Christopher Maurer,
Brookline, Massachusetts,
October 2021

ix   **Prologue.** First published by Verónica Cortínez as "Notes on Carlos Germán Belli," *Plaza: Revista de Literatura* (Harvard University) 12 (spring 1987): 39-46. In March 2015, discussing a "handsome" essay on Belli by Mario Vargas Llosa, "a pleasure to read" ("Carlos Germán Belli: don de poesía," *VJ*, pp. 5-7), it occurred to Karl that his own introduction to Belli, written so many years before ("but it seems like yesterday") was "not superfluous" and, though his understanding of Belli had deepened, could serve as prologue to this book: "surely, I said there some things that need to be said. Of course I'd be glad not to exhume it!— *if* there exists another essay where someone else says it better. Or if *you* could say it better. If you ever sense a lucky hour, in which you could pin some of these things down, I wish you would" (KM, 3/28/2015). I couldn't and haven't. I have included Karl's essay here not as a map of Belli's poetry, but because these pages tell us memorably about Belli's style and some of his main themes, the challenges of translating him, and—above all, what is less common—they pulse with the love of one poet for another.

El nudo / The Knot (p. xx). *VJ*, 419. From *Bajo el sol de la medianoche rojo* (1990). KM made several versions of this poem.

Asir la forma que se va / Taking Hold of the Form That Flees (p. 2). *VJ* 633. This paragraph serves as epilogue in the 2007 edition of *Sextinas, villanelas y baladas*. See also *Morar* 285. Published in *Ouragora*, March 26, 2008, along with three poems of Belli ("Hare-Lip", "The Extraterrestrials", "To My Brother"), with an audio recording.

Poema (Nuestro amor no está) / Poem (Our love is not) (p. 4). *VJ* 13. "This particular poem is one of the very few (only two or three; 'Labio leporino' is another) in which, from dislike of 'filler', I didn't try to mime his meter exactly, but made some lines shorter than his. E.g. line 2 *'y castos genitales, nuestro amor'* (5 feet) = 'chaste genitals, our love' (3 feet). But even when I do that, English still needs *iambs*, and cannot have missing or extra syllables that make it non-iambic—for then it becomes mere free verse—and that, I think, breaks the metrical spell" (KM, 2/20/2015). Line 6 *esperan/* expect: could also mean "hope."

Variaciones para mi hermano Alfonso / Variations for My Brother Alfonso (p. 6). *VJ* 21. KM translated only the first two sections of this five-part poem of Belli to his brother Alfonso, and never finished section 2. Asked in 2011 about the dark vision of human life in his early books, Belli responded, "Without a doubt, my brother Alfonso, an invalid from birth, has been the reason I perceive the human condition as disabled. I became his legal caretaker when our mother passed away in 1957. With time I came to consider myself his twin. Curiously, in Cajamarca, at a literary event […] I read a poem dedicated to him, as I always did in public readings, but this time it was like a premonitory goodbye: hours later he died in Lima. I think the pain I felt as brother refined, and surely gave rise to, my literary vocation and clearly it was the principal cause of that peculiar vision of humanity." Francisco José Cruz, "Carlos Germán Belli, un converso *sui generis*," http://franciscojosecruz.blogspot.com, 6/8/2011.

Una desconocida voz / An Unknown Voice (p. 8). *VJ* 57.

¡Oh padres, sabedlo bien…! / O parents, know this well! (p. 10), *VJ* 65.

En saliendo del vientre / In leaping from the womb (p. 12), VJ 66.

En Bética no bella / In Unbeautiful Baetis (p. 14). *VJ* 93. "Unbeautiful Baetis": Lima as reimagined through the reading of sixteenth- and seventeenth-century poets—including pastoral poets—of Seville, the Roman Baetica. Belli's favorites, perhaps, were Francisco de Medrano, Fernando de Herrera, Andrés Fernández de Andrada (author of the "Epístola moral a Fabio") and Rodrigo Caro, who wrote an ode to the Roman ruins of Italica. Belli's voice, "though intimately of his time and place, is strange to it, because it reaches thrillingly far back into the past. It unites a present living voice with the voices of the dead. And in that way it (a) makes those come to life again and (b) gives the present a strange, queer depth; it's as if it had been suddenly touched by eternity. And that is 'poetic power' (KM to Verónica Cortínez, 11/4/2009). *Crudos* in line 1 preserves its older Spanish sense of "cruel" and *abolladuras* (line 3) are "dents," as in metal.

A mi hermano Alfonso / To My Brother Alfonso (p. 16). *VJ* 103. *desalada Austro:* "I thought maybe he's recalling the Latin South Wind, which is always violent, stormy, etc.)" (KM to CM, 8/3/14). "I think he likes ending the poem on the Gongorine noun *nada* as in that sonnet '*Mientras por competir por tu cabello...*' [...] There's a kind of gradation...descending from harshness to emptiness to nothingness: harsh, vain, or eternally nothing" (CM to KM 8/3/2014).

Poema (Frunce el feto su frente) / Poem (The foetus screws his face) (p. 18). *VJ* 106.

Labio leporino / Hare-lip (p. 20). *VJ* 121. "Here I did not try to keep the original lineation. But notice how instructive this is: The first four lines of Spanish [have far more syllables] yet I excised almost nothing" (KM, 2/23/2015) In other versions, he translated "desalado" (literally, de-salted, un-salted or de-winged) in line 6 as "uneasy." In Belli, *desalado* also seems to mean quick or fast (like a hare, bird or airplane) or nimbly, like a poet knitting words together.

La tortilla / The Omelette (p. 22). *VJ* 123.

Robot sublunar / Sublunary Robot (p. 24). *VJ* 133. Line 24: "Doom-filled tomorrow": more literally, "inescapable tomorrow," "ineluctable tomorrow."

Por el monte abajo / Down the Mountain (p. 26). *VJ* 137. In an unpublished note on Belli (ca. 1987), KM writes: "When a poet's art (e.g., that of Mandelstam) is derived from spontaneous living speech, the single verse is the basic unit of thought. Belli's more 'literary' art loves the stanza. He satisfies his hunger for the spoken word by using brief exclamations—exclamatory adverbial remarks—that are grammatically subordinate but which often have an independent, almost epigrammatic power. He also uses adverbial particles (*ya, bien que, ahora, cual, cuánto*, etc.) sometimes in tense little clusters, which recall the spoken word even though they have a strict logical function. Where Belli says '*por este monte abajo cuánto agudo*,' we sense the germ, the undifferentiated embryo of a great aphorism (all its organs are there but the verb is still in the womb of thought.) We sense a very complex period but also an exclamation! / His message, that of a modern Job, is far simpler than that of most other poets. This is one reason for the complexity of his syntax, which is always ironical. Belli soon discovered that stereoscopic Latinate syntax—which, in the manner of Góngora, examines every object from all sides, as if poking at it and probing it with the stick of thought—is an excellent device for conveying the emptiness, the harshness of an 'external world' from which God has absconded. He is so in love with this method, based on a paradox, that he never abandons it."

Los estigmas / The Stigmas (p. 28). *VJ* 144. In line 2, *coche*, Karl preferred "coach" to "car" and in line 13 (*su gobierno*) took the possessive to mean "its" (the truck's) rather than "their" (the headlights').

Silva antibiótica / Antibiotic Silva (p. 300). *VJ* 146. The *silva*, which combines verses of 7 and 11 Spanish syllables, is one of Belli's favorite verse forms, handed down from 16th and 17th-century Spanish poets from Garcilaso to Góngora.

El uso del talon / The Use of the Heel (p. 32). *VJ* 147.

Los extraterrestres / The Extraterrestrials (p. 34). *VJ* 152.

Canción primera / First Song (p. 36). *VJ* 157-158. One of Belli's enduring loves in poetry is the *canzone* of Petrarch. KM writes, "It seems incredible that ["First Song"] was written over 45 years ago. It's so strange how dense and deep and nearly perfect his art was almost from the very beginning. It's astonishing too how little the 'message' has changed. It was then a ferocious protest, against the impossible conditions of earthly existence; it's now a continuous astonishment at the impossible, yet actual, nearness of bliss. But the ferocious protest was [so] full of gigantic tact, self-restraint, and humor, that it foresaw *el buen mudar* long before it happened; and the present happiness repudiates nothing of the protests. It relates them with the utmost courtesy—even using their very words—just from courtesy and attentiveness, and to make them happier" (KM to CM, 2/22/2015). "His masculine endings tend to have great force and skill. For example, notice the Envoi. It has 2 trimeters, a pentameter, and 3 trimeters; but the first two trimeters have feminine endings; the last three, all masculine. Did you notice? My translation imitated that" (KM to CM, 2/28/2015). "Strophe II actually has no main verb—it's just a pendant to strope I, which ends with an 'if-clause': str. II just adds another if-clause. (So that at the end of str. I he could have put a comma instead of a period)" (KM to CM, 2/24/2015).

"In strophe III, I want the dashes in the first and penultimae lines, to show that throughout the stanza 'the clay' is waiting for its verb ('may well be')" (KM to CM, 3/12/2015).

Los engranajes / The Transmissions (p. 40). *VJ* 171-172, with a dedication to the Argentine poet Enrique Molina (1910-1997), with whose vision of a womb-like prenatal paradise, and coming-to-less upon birth, Belli has expressed affinity. The title might be more literally translated as "The Gears" or "The Cogs in the Machine."

Sextina de los desiguales / Sestina of the Unequals (p. 44). *VJ* 173-174. "It's one of the deftest sestinas I've ever seen. They almost always 'drag' and ramble. Belli's doesn't because he had the brilliant idea of using three pairs of opposites: Donkey feeling hopeless love for a Mare; Elm tree ditto for a Rose; Daylight ditto for the Night. The third of course is brilliant all by itself, since it reverses the more usual theme, 'Follow thy fair Sun, unhappy shadow'. In Belli it's 'Follow thy sweet Night, unhappy Day!' But I remember that Spanish sonnet I once translated [by Francisco de la Torre, one of Belli's favorite poets], that begins: 'You with your cape of stars I follow, / Silence, whom lights transparent throng, / Foe of the Muses' lord Apollo, / Nocturnal bird of ominous song'" ("Sigo, silencio, tu estrellado manto / de transparentes lumbres guarnecido. / enemiga del Sol esclarecido, / ave nocturna de agorero canto") (KM to CM, 3/6/15.) Belli discovered the sextina reading "Sestina: Altaforte" of Ezra Pound, and followed it through Arnaut Daniel, Dante, Petrarch, and 16th- and 17th-century Spaniards.

La cara de mis hijas / The Face of My Daughters (p. 48). *VJ* 179. "What do you think of [...] using rhyme for a rhymeless poem? And also shrinking each line by 1 foot. [...] Every other way I try with this one, definitely doesn't work. Some poems are just not translatable. As always in Belli, the faintly archaic diction is so fiendishly subtle! Notice that what it really is is an unrhymed sonnet, with an octet and a sestet)" (KM to CM, 5/15/2010).

Boda de la pluma y la letra / Wedding of the Pen and the Letter (p. 50) *VJ* 212-213. In his essay on "El sexo en el texto" ("Sex in the Text") Belli observes that "words harmoniously strung together are truly closer—in the act of reading—than the muse lying in bed. And one feels that the fire of life burns just as bright in the verbal body: sensual pleasure, esthetic pleasure, and sex indissolubly united in the text. [...] The word is pure pulp, and thanks to art it can assume the loveliness of well-rounded thighs, breasts, and hips. The letter is the essence of the divine pulp, fecundated night after night by the phallic quill, which, in the case of [Rubén Darío] is not that of a somber owl, but that of an aristocratic swan." (*Morar*, 216). Karl asked me to annotate the antepenultimate line with its play of meaning: "no longer chilly *bridal chamber*"; but *cámara frigorífica* can mean cold storage, refrigeration room. "Regarding that perfect and untranslatable pun, 'en la nupcial cámara ya no frigorífica,'— I suppose that for stuff like that we should have notes, no? (I suppose, end notes, not footnotes; perhaps all at the end of the book.) And plainly it should be *you* who write them. About this I have a bit of strong advice, which is, to make these notes now, as we go along. I.e., whenever you see (or sense) that a note is needed, try to write it up at once very formally, very 'camera-ready' (even with all the citations, if any). This is what I do with [Jacob] Balde—I often pause even in the middle of translating to do it. For if one leaves the notes all till later, that work becomes huge and oppressive, and one does it worse. They can later of course be emended, and some excised; but that work is so easy and rapid, it's not even work but fun. (Whereas making all the notes at once from scratch is so un-fun, that this is why my *Georgics* translation is still lying in my desk, when it should have been published ten years ago)" (KM to CM 4/14/2015). In line 6 of strophe IV, *de la prenda dueño*, "I think this means the now-empowered black pen, hence my semicolon; if you really think it means the Swan, then after 'Swan' put not a semicolon but a comma" (KM to CM, 4/1/2015).

Mi victoria / My Victory (p. 54). *VJ* 307. Written in *liras*, another of the verse forms Belli inherits from 16th-century Spaniards (Garcilaso, but also fray Luis de León, a poet of longing, like Belli): stanzas of five lines of 7 and 11 Spanish syllables.

Las migajuelas del Rey Sumerio / The Crumbs of the Sumerian King (p. 56). *VJ* 316-318. On a trip to New York, after looking at avant-garde art in the Museum of Modern Art and the Sumerian art at the Metropolitan, Belli could not help thinking that "almost all the bread of the spirit was eaten at the dawn of humanity, and that the power of creation was exhausted with the Sumerians, who developed the arts of architecture and sculpture exceptionally well and who, beside, gave the world a true present: writing" (*Morar* 320). In a note, in 2014, KM observed that Belli's verse "has a kind of solitude, caused in part by its apparent self-absorption. Its basic method was invented many decades ago. The formal addictions of his youth are still present. Even images recur. Very late verse alludes to very early, or even quotes it verbatim, and seems a meditation on it. Yet the meaning changes deeply. A late poem echoes an earlier, but is like a revelation of its real meaning. As an odd consequence of this, the first retains its full radiance. Compare, for example, 'Por el monte abajo' (1966) with 'Las migajuelas del Rey Sumerio' (1986), or compare 'Labio leporino' (1966) with '¡Salve Spes!' (2002). Though in different meters, and though the second says almost the exact opposite of the first, they are at heart the same poem: and each is a masterpiece, never to be superseded."

El buen mudar / The Good Change (p. 62). *VJ* 325-326.

El nido codiciado / The Coveted Nest (p. 66). *VJ* 327. In an email, KM tells his friend Roberto Castillo, who had sent him a literal translation, that "El nido codiciado" "seems suddenly clear like daylight. For plainly man—and precisely the

man who searches 'con gran porfía'—forever 'claws' the line of
the horizon thinking that happiness lies there. [...] He ran-
sacks all creation. He searches amid the stars and amid the
atoms, or in Thucydides, or claws the equally empty 'horizon'
of a perfect rhyme. / Thus the 'dragon' is only an image of his
'gran porfía.' [... The] dragon suddenly turns to a little bird.
I.e. our longing itself turns to a vision of the nest, for which
it has been 'scraping' throughout the poem. / What causes
this? To put it theologically, Belli is orthodox and believes
in Grace, rewarding a search [...] All this reminds me of one
Brave Buffalo who said c. 1838: 'when I was 10 years old
I looked at the land and the rivers, the sky above, and the
animals around me and could not fail to realize that they
were made by some great power. I was so anxious to under-
stand this power that I questioned the trees and the bushes.
[[Here, the dragon is clawing the horizon.]] It seemed as
though the flowers were staring at me, and I wanted to
ask them 'Who made you?' I looked at the moss-covered
stones, some of them seemed to have the features of a man,
but they could not answer me. Then I had a dream [[here,
Grace cometh]] and in my dream one of these small round
stones appeared to me and told me that the maker of all
was Wakan-Tanka [the 'Great Spirit,' Sioux word for God],
and that in order to honor him I must honor his works in
nature. The stone said that by my search I had shown myself
worthy of supernatural help. It said that if I were curing a
sick person I might ask its assistance, said that all the forces
of nature would help me work a cure.' / That is not panthe-
ism; it's what happens in Belli's poem; for in his dream, at
last, the clawed dragon learns—simply, is told!—that the
world was made by God. That the world was not the place
for his fierce search, but the nest of his happiness. And that
there pure abundance was any straw or humble stone. / For
in order to feel the full force of what Brave Buffalo is saying,
you have to know that he really did work cures, and that he
found out how to do it by talking (literally) with leaves, or
stones; and that he indeed lived on mere crumbs."

No salir jamás / Never to go out any more (p. 68). *VJ* 418.
Line 10: or "in her, thus, to be curdled, body and soul".

Las cosas de la casa / The Things of the House (p. 70). *VJ*
443. Line 10: the meaning is, "for as day and night go by...".
Templado can mean moderate in food and drink—KM's
"abstemious"—but line 13 might also be translated "in the
warm bosom of the house."

Recuerdo de hermano / Memory of My Brother (p. 72).
VJ 444-445. Karl thought this poem "the most beautiful
poem that I have ever read in any language" (KM to CM,
1/7/2009).

¡Salve, Spes! / Salve, Spes! (p. 76). *VJ* 459-462. The first
section of a ten-part poem. In an essay Belli observes that
hope "seems a common, prosaic, super-trite thing, just barely
worthy of some simple little popular song—poor, slobbered
over. However that may be, let us head resolutely in her
direction, rescue her from the swamp into which she has
sunk up to her eyebrows, nearly drowning in the mucky
waters of everyday existence, and let's give her something
like mouth to mouth resuscitation, so she can go on living,
her little heart beating, or—better—pealing like a resonant
bell." (*Morar* 139)

¡Salve, Spes! IX / Salve Spes! IX (p. 84). *VJ* 491-494.
Section 9 of a ten-part poem, with an epigraph from the
Mauritian Malcolm de Chazal (1902-1981), "artist, vision-
ary and mystic, a rare combination today," who considered
"the paroxysm of lovemaking the greatest means of access to
the other world" and raised "voluptuousness" to the meta-
physical (see Belli's essay in *Morar* 233-35).

**Al pintor Giovanni Donato da Montorfano [1440-1510]
/ To the Painter Giovanni Donato da Montorfano [1440-
1510]** (p. 92). *VJ* 517-519. In an essay Belli notes how

the crowds looking at Leonardo's *Last Supper* turn their backs—literally and disdainfully—on Donato da Montorfano's fresco *The Crucifixion*, on another wall of the refectory of Santa Maria delle Grazie, Milan. He is "truly orphaned" (*Morar* 371). KM writes to CM, à propos of an anthology of 20th-century Latin American poetry which did not include Belli: "But really, that's just what people are like. They're very astoundingly blind, unless you put a spell on them—and keep renewing the spell. Contemplating the fate of Belli always makes me think of a translated line from Rilke that I read once 45 years ago and never forgot. He [wrote] about the quiet 'imperturbable' carvers of stone in the medieval cathedral, statues so high up that no one would ever see them, that quietly 'carved themselves into the constant stone' ('For Wolf Graf von Kalckreuth')."

Cavilación del caminante / The Walker's Perplexity (p. 98). *VJ* 589-590. KM, March 28, 2015. "I once read somewhere that Housman thought that English iambic tetrameter must always rhyme; he thought that without rhyme it isn't even verse, only free verse. But I think he's wrong. I find the 'meter' of this translation rather fascinatingly musical (whatever its other defects, or errors). Hardest to translate seems the title. Every literal translation I try seems clunky; so I gave it a Hardy-like title. [...] But what a good poem—no?! In modern times it's very, very, very rare, or more than rare, to find poems like these of Belli, that simply, sensitively, and with such purity of language, record utter bafflement at the human condition (or rather, sublunar condition, since he worries about other creatures too)—but does it without anger, without a Yeatsian or Rilke-like oration about it, but as quietly as Mozart. For things as pure, you have to go all the way back to Anyte, or Simonides! But Hardy now and then comes close, [for example, in "An August Midnight" and "Winter Night in Woodland (Old Time)"].

Cuando los estorbos se van / When the Obstacles Vanish
(p. 102). *VJ* 597. Line 18: Literally, "of him who believed
that all was in darkness." Final two lines: Literally, "as though
living in advance / the eternity that is [now] close."

Swan Isle Press is a not-for-profit literary and academic publisher of fiction, nonfiction, and poetry.

For information on books of related interest or for a catalog of new publications contact: www.swanislepress.com

The Azure Cloister | Thirty-Five Poems
Designed by Marianne Jankowski
Typeset in Adobe Jenson Pro
Printed on 55# Natural Offset Antique